# MIRACULOUS

# MIRACULOUS

## NAVIGATING THE COVID-19 STORM: A FIVE-YEAR JOURNEY, PASTOR AND WIFE'S ACCOUNT OF ILLNESS AND RECOVERY

### EXTENDED EDITION

**GEORGE F. AND LILA A. DEFORD**

G. Franklin DeFord, Publisher
Pomfret, MD 20675
Copyright © 2025 by George F. DeFord
All Rights Reserved

*MIRACULOUS:*
*Navigating The COVID-19 Storm: A Five-Year Journey*
*A Pastor and Wife's Account of Illness and Recovery*
EXTENDED EDITION

Inquiries and permission to reproduce material from this work should be addressed to:

Rev. Dr. George F. DeFord at brownbay67@gmail.com

All Scripture quotations, unless otherwise noted, are taken from the New Revised Standard Version (NRSV) 2003 by Abingdon Press, Nashville, Tennessee.

Disclaimer

Manufactured in the United States of America
Book Cover design: Visions That Transcend
Cataloging-in-Publication data is available from the Library of Congress.
ISBN: 979-8-218-82704-5 (paperback)
E-ISBN: 979-8-218-82705-2 (ebook)

# ENDORSEMENTS

Since the horrific effects of COVID-19, there have been many recounts, stories, and memoirs written to share this unique period of world history, but none more impactful than this one by Reverend George and Lila DeFord. Their unique perspective is undergirded by George DeFord's ability to remember and articulate specific details in spite of being hospitalized and isolated for a month and in rehabilitation for several weeks. Further, the detailed diary kept by Lila during this entire experience, while she herself had the virus, is amazing. Undergirding all their work is their comprehensive knowledge and trust in the Holy Bible and complete trust in Jesus Christ, whose resurrection was a "Miracle". I commend this unique memoir, which could prove to be a classic for future times.

—Bishop Forrest C. Stith, Retired,
The United Methodist Church

Rev. Dr. George and Mrs. Lila DeFord provide a deep river of the power of miracles, prayer, fasting, and healing. Their Memoir, *Miraculous,* is a first-person account of their journey through the dark pandemic valley of COVID-19. It brings to light the voices and testimony of over 26

million Americans who lived in the valley of death and uncertainty [in those early days]. Their work will provide a vision to all who know that faith doesn't make things easy … it makes them possible. A must-read for all who know that "our time under God is NOW".
—Rev. Dr. Bernard Keels, Retired Dean,
Morgan State University Memorial Chapel


*"Miraculous"* is one couple's compelling and inspirational testimony about the power of prayer and their determination to survive Coronavirus. This candid narrative with vivid descriptions of sickness and recovery is a must-read for all people of faith.
—Joshua K. Wright, Ph.D., Associate Professor of History,
Trinity Washington University, Washington, DC


A million died and he was almost one of them, but the Reverend George DeFord, through prayer and God's will, was wheeled OUT of the hospital on a gurney through the front door 30 days after he arrived, as dozens of staff cheered his survival.

Their book [George and Lila DeFord] tells the story that so many others never lived to tell of fears and confusion as an airborne disease began to consume their bodies. George tells of life on a ventilator and how so many things that were so important on the schedule of a busy pastor ceased to matter at all. If you want a detailed inside look at COVID from one who almost joined the ancestors, then I would recommend this book.
—Sam Ford, WJLA TV Washington, DC reporter, retired

Rev. Dr. George DeFord, a retired United Methodist Pastor, is a critical and theological thinker, and a scholarly and prolific writer. Through the years, he authored several books relating to his experiences during his pastorate of congregations in urban, suburban, and rural settings, such as his book relative to the grief experiences of clergy families (including his own). His book, titled *Miraculous* [its first edition], is an account of his near-death encounter with COVID-19, which he faced in the early months of 2020.

The reader of *MIRACULOUS*, the *Extended Edition*, rendering five years of revelation, is drawn into a miraculous experience relative to the power of fervent, community-centered prayer. Mrs. Lila DeFord assumed the role of a prayer warrior and enlisted a community of believers in prayer for the deliverance of Dr. DeFord. Meanwhile, during his hospital stay, Dr. DeFord was placed on a ventilator.

MIRACULOUSLY, after many weeks, Dr. DeFord was healed, delivered, and released from the hospital on May 8, 2020, reassuring the people of God that prayer still works.

Truly, the words of James became a reality to all who engaged in the prayer endeavor as we lifted Dr. DeFord's condition before the Lord: "The prayer of a person living right with God is something powerful to be reckoned with." James 5:16b (The Message).

Additionally, any person who reads MIRACULOUS is brought into the reality of what Edward M. Bounds describes in *The Possibilities of Prayer*: "IT is the answer to prayer which brings praying out of the realm of dry, dead things and makes praying a thing of life and power."

Finally, I recommend *MIRACULOUS: Navigating The COVID-19 Storm: A Five-Year Journey, A Pastor and Wife's Account of Illness and Recovery, EXTENDED EDITION* as a must-read resource for any and all believers during this period of skepticism, faith-stretching, and faith-shaking times.

—Rev. Dr. Eugene Matthews, Retired, District Superintendent, Baltimore Washington Conference, United Methodist Church

*Dedicated to:*
MARGARET C. S. MCRAE, MOTHER
*1923-2020*
&
*The Medical Teams*
*of the University of Maryland Charles Regional Medical Center*

# TABLE OF CONTENTS

# FOREWORD

*Miraculous* [Extended Edition] is an extraordinary personal chronicling of a fierce battle and conquest over COVID-19 that, for a time, signaled Goliath-like encroachment of ultimate incapacitation and death. My wife and I received news of our friends' plight in disbelief. *Miraculous* is a testimony of souls leaning on God's protective care and consoling grace. Mrs. Lila DeFord's persevering in prayer and fasting has brought to mind profound searching thoughts of Dr. Howard Thurman in his *Meditations of the Heart* (pp. 184—185):

"Who has not stood beside the tragedy of a loved one and not been paralyzed by the sheer impotence and helplessness of love …? Something surely can be done, but what? There must be help available, but where? There must be an answer, but how to find it?

"The Word from the Book is: 'Cast all your care upon God, for He careth for you.'

This is no idle word—no mere utterance of piety nestled in a great fear. This is the Word of courage and of faith."

Affirmative care-casting resonates deeply, from beginning to end, as the heartthrob of courageous faith. Prayer and fasting (disciples of tarrying and conversing with the Divine pain-bearer who, in our affliction, is afflicted, as the Book so awesomely reassures us) fed and emboldened trust in God's healing embrace.

*Miraculous* is written with Rev. Dr. DeFord's characteristic penchant for patiently crafted reminiscence. Insightful, accessible definitions of biblical words, snapshots of clinical data, celebratory mention of healthcare workers (their compassionate vigilance and the openly expressed faith of a few), the empathy of friends, colleagues, parishioners, and the devoted care loved ones provided are presented here with love's strong glow of grateful hearts.

More than chronicling, more than moving reflections sprung from faithful hearts of beloved souls, *Miraculous* is an invitation to readers to cast all their care upon the One whose mercies cannot be numbered and who could not care more.

Finally, I dream of a time when historians will turn to the story that unfolds in these pages and the testimonies of others and discover that uncovering the anatomy of the hopes and fears of the present in the war against COVID-19 yields fresh insight into the resilience of the human spirit as the true heritage of the race.

—THE REVEREND OBIE WRIGHT, JR., RETIRED MEMBER, BALTIMORE WASHINGTON CONFERENCE, THE UNITED METHODIST CHURCH

# ACKNOWLEDGMENTS

We owe a debt of gratitude to the medical staff of the University of Maryland Charles Regional Medical Center in La Plata, Maryland. While we cannot name each from the Emergency Room (ER) to the Quarantine area and Intensive Care Unit (ICU), the members demonstrated exemplarily professional training and technical skills notwithstanding their compassion and empathy for my physical well-being, so I could recover from this "nasty straph" (Staphylococcus infection) virus as my high school chum, Rev. Dr. Emora Brannon described it. Also unforgettable in my mind is the spirituality of the unnamed nurses who said to me, "We prayed for you," and Ms. LaTisha Williams of environmental services, who daily prayed over me. And to Dr. Young and others who navigated my treatments in the ICU, we are eternally grateful to God for you.

Lila and I are especially thankful to Ms. Karen, ICU Coordinator, for her diligence in keeping my wife updated on my physical condition during the bout with COVID-19 and hospital send-off. Case Manager Ms. Lori Parson, who assisted with my transfer to a rehabilitation facility. Mr. Joe Stein, a Nurse Manager, ICU, and Mr. Craig Renner, Director, Marketing & Communications, University of Maryland,

Charles Regional Medical Center, for their assistance in clarifying hospital policies and authorizations of certain photographs.

In this extended edition of *Miraculous*, we wanted to be sure to convey our appreciation to Mary Hannah, VP of Population Health and Case Manager, and Teri White, a Transitional Nurse Navigator, who not only participated in my recovery, but also, it was an honor to re-engage with them five years later. They remembered me!

We are indebted to Rev. Dr. Johnsie Cogman, Washington East District, District Superintendent, Baltimore-Washington Conference, The United Methodist Church, for shepherding Smith Chapel UMC, while the DeFord Family was in the midst of the Coronavirus storm, and Dr. Cogman was ultimately able to guide this local church to receive a new pastor, Keith White, while tending to the spiritual needs of our family. The transition was seamless as the lay ministers carried out their ministries without difficulty. We are thankful for Dr. Cogman's comments in our memoir.

We were moved by the many expressions of love, condolences, and sympathy from the members of Smith Chapel UMC, particularly the leadership, including the Certified Lay Ministers: Audrey Chase, Rachel Stewart-Johnson, Jocelyn Richardson, and Perry Taylor. Also, Lay Leader Vera Littlejohn and Veronica "Elenora" Milstead, Chair of Church Council, who checked on Lila by phone and/or email, in addition to "Jackie" and "Pete" Williams. From the "kitchen crew", that is to say, Almalita, Mrs. Dorothy, Gail, Phyllis, "Aunt Frost", Iretha, and Nancy gave their reactions to our sickness with COVID-19, and mentioned in this memoir.

We will be forever grateful to our clergy friends who made weekly telephone calls to check on my status and Lila's; they also responded with cards and emails. Reverends Eugene Matthews, Stephen Tillette, and Obie Wright gave written reactions to our illness.

Lila and I are forever indebted to the ever-persistent Prayer and Praise Warriors (PPW), a group initially lovingly comprised of two members of Westphalia Christian Community Church (a UMC congregation): Mrs. Gwendolyn Kent and First Lady Stephanie West, and soon, joined by my wife. Before long, the PPW grew by an additional member, Johanna Coleman, the wife of photographer Dwight Coleman. Additionally, I'd like to thank Rev. Dr. Timothy West, Senior Pastor of Westphalia, for his support.

We thank the many members from other congregations who sent us get-well cards, some of whom we knew and a few of whom were unknown congregants from other churches, some of whom are included in this memoir.

My classmates of *Morgan State University Class of 1967 (Soulful Centennials)* and the MSU Southern Maryland Alumni Chapter were thoughtful in their reactions and expressions of care for Lila and me.

I thank my fraternity brothers of Phi Beta Sigma Fraternity, Incorporated, Zeta Chi Sigma Chapter of Prince George's County, Maryland, for checking on my family's well-being and for Bro. Willie Harrison, who called a number of times to offer landscaping during my absence, and Bro. Gerard Moore, who supervises nurses in the ICU in another hospital. Bro. Moore explained the procedures involved in treatments such as intubation to my wife, Lila.

Mrs. Gloria Turner-Simpkins did a phenomenal job of preliminary editing and proofreading our initial work, offering valuable suggestions.

We deeply appreciate our clergy colleagues and friends for their support and endorsements in the persons of: Rev. Dr. Bernard Keels, former Dean of Morgan State Memorial Chapel, Bishop Forrest C. Stith, Retired, The United Methodist Church, and Dr. Joshua Wright, Associate Professor, Trinity Washington University, who endorsed our work, and The Reverend Obie Wright submitted the Foreword.

We thank our family for their submitted reactions to our plight with COVID-19, and especially Dante, who is our Guardian Angel in human flesh, who watches over his aging senior parents. Also, Sheila Schofield, sister, readily responded to our requests for preliminary drafts of segments from both the original and extended editions of our book.

We thank Yvonne J. Medley of Medley Management and Prose, Inc., for her inestimable professional assistance and editing expertise while navigating us through this revised extended edition, which would not have been possible without her.

Lila and I thank ALMIGHTY GOD for hearing and answering prayers for a situation that seemed impossible but miraculously turned because of God's grace and healing mercies. Thanks be to God!

REV. DR. GEORGE F. AND LILA A. DEFORD
RETIRED PASTOR AND WIFE

# PREFACE

We write this memoir to share our firsthand experiences as a pastoral family that suffered the horrific Coronavirus disease in the early spring of 2020. This Extended Edition shares five years of reflections on an experience—shared with the world—that changed our perspectives, assumptions, and what we take for granted—or not—from this moment forward.

The impact of the disease drastically changed our lifestyle with the death of Mother Margaret McRae, my wife's mother, and my mother-in-love, and an unexpected but necessary relinquishing of an eight-year pastoral ministry with a congregation that my wife, Lila, and I loved serving during our retirement years. Our circumstances could be likened, to some degree, to those of the biblical character Job, who encountered a series of calamities that threatened to shake his faith. But God, the Great I am, delivered and led us through the wilderness of darkness and uncertainty.

A personal account of my journey as a pastor, who suffered the potentially deadly effects of the COVID-19 storm during its early phase in Southern Maryland, is shared, in addition to poignant flashes of consciousness while a patient in the ICU of the University of Maryland Charles Regional Medical Center in LaPlata, Maryland. The paradox of feeling close yet distant from my mother-in-law, who passed away without her immediate family by her side, has left a lasting impression of traumatic pain that persists to this day.

I endeavor to present biblical and theological definitions of the term *miracle*. My conviction that miracles are still operant in the twenty-first century is part of my affirmation of faith as a Christian minister and servant of the Lord Jesus Christ.

Lila, my wife, shares her personal reactions and the chronology of her daily, tenacious practice of praying and fasting, along with two special sisters in Christ who became cognizant of our circumstances. Her candid sharing opens the reader into the spirit of a pastor's wife during a very difficult moment in her family's life.

We present in this revised and extended edition of *Miraculous* a collection of words of comfort, encouragement, and hope for our recovery and well-being from the horrific COVID-19 Global Pandemic of 2020. Furthermore, the softly edited sentiments are presented for the reader.

I offer reflections through the lens of the Holy Scripture about my journey through the storm, and reliance upon the Word of God is indisputable.

I embark upon an extension of our work by recalling episodes from my childhood days, along with my late sister, Brenda, when our maternal grandmother cared for us while our mother worked. Significantly, the memory of a certain loud thunderstorm and its echoes, which caused the two of us to be very fearful and quiet while God spoke, as we were told, surfaced. The lingering aftermath of the COVID-19 Global Pandemic reminded me of the echoes from the loud thunderstorm of my childhood.

Many institutions and organizations, including the church, initiated precautionary measures to prevent the spread of the deadly coronavirus. To this end, many agencies and groups established protocols to preclude the spread of the virus. Now five years out and counting, while some have rescinded certain precautionary measures, others remain in place as the norm, i.e., face coverings, less handshaking and hugging, more bottles of sanitizing liquid—popping out of purses and pockets—and thorough, concentrated efforts when it comes to washing hands (which should have always been the norm).

Anecdotal to the positive effects of the Global Pandemic, I write about collateral blessings that nudged our children to become active in the ministries of the church. While my battle with COVID-19 eventually forced me to retire from my pastoral leadership at Smith Chapel United Methodist Church in Pisgah, Maryland, Lila and I welcomed new opportunities to serve in ministries with Westphalia Christian Community Church in Upper Marlboro, Maryland.

Finally, I offer closing thoughts and revelations about our journey, now five years removed from the initial trauma experienced by millions of other non-immunized persons caught in the early storm of the COVID-19 Global Pandemic. While so many—young and old, healthy and those challenged by pre-existing conditions, God believers and nonbelievers—perished—how is it that I was spared? I have tried to address this question within the concept of a *Miracle*. This account, presented in the following chapters, is also open to the reader's stark interpretation. God still miraculously heals using the work of dedicated medical professionals and scientists. Therefore, while I want this *Extended Edition* of our book, *Miraculous*, to fuel your faith and fight to prevail over any future storms, I also welcome the debate.

Why and how was I miraculously delivered by God's grace and healing mercies?

Thanks be to God for God's indescribable gift [healing mercies] (2 Corinthians 9:15). Amen!

# INTRODUCTION

The Coronavirus (COVID-19) is an insidious disease that has caused illnesses and deaths of millions of people in a worldwide pandemic. The COVID-19 Global Pandemic's epicenter was in China, with a subsequent impact on countries such as South Korea, Japan, Iran, Italy, Spain, and Germany, among others. The disease eventually spread to the United States during the first part of 2020. Asian and European countries effectively managed the COVID-19 pandemic through strategies of facial coverings, mandatory quarantines, social distancing, and washing of hands. Moreover, the said strategies were non-political statements, while in America, the practices became demonized as political statements.

Pandemics are not new or unique to human history. The death rate due to the deadly COVID-19 disease still astounds us. Kohelet (the Preacher or Teacher) around 250 BCE wrote: "There is nothing new under the sun" (Ecclesiastes 1:9) The Black Plague, 1346-1353, Cholera 1817-1824, Spanish Influenza, 1918-1920, SARS, 2002-2004, and the Ebola Pandemic 2013-2016, in each case, health care workers took positive steps to eliminate the plagues. With the aid of available medical knowledge, medical scientists and physicians responded effectively, achieving positive outcomes that led to the healing of many patients. Sadly, there were still too many who died of COVID-19 in the United States, primarily because of the failures of effective leadership in the national government and the failure to put practice-proven strategies that could have curtailed the spread of the deadly virus during 2020 and early 2021.

The United States has the disesteem of leading the world in the incidence of coronavirus cases, which is reported to be three million-plus as we write and reevaluate, five years out, the account of our illness and recovery from COVID-19 during the spring of 2020. The death rate reported by the Center for Disease Control (CDC) was 400,000 plus. Such data suggest a dismal and hopeless situation for Americans of every ethnic, socio-economic, age group, and academic level.

The State of Maryland had 11,696 Coronavirus cases with a mortality rate of 3,790. Included in the state's statistics of COVID-19 cases and deaths were Charles County's data of 2,725 and 97, respectively, as reported in the *Southern Maryland News, Friday, September 25, 2020, page 5*. Data reflected in *Worldometer*, pertinent to Maryland, updated on December 6, 2020, showed: 215,027 Coronavirus Cases; 4,846 Deaths; 8,785 Recoveries. As of December 17, 2020, *The New York Times* revealed 246,190 known Coronavirus cases and 5,368 deaths in Maryland: Charles County, with 5,323 cases and 115 deaths. It was within this pandemic milieu that my wife and I suffered from the infection of the Coronavirus.

I took a proactive measure on March 8, 2020, by having Minister Rachel S. Johnson, RN, give a special presentation to the congregation regarding precautions against COVID-19, which was beginning to infect citizens, especially in New York. Minister Johnson demonstrated the proper way to thoroughly wash hands, including the recommended length of time to perform the safety measure, which is approximately the time it takes to sing the popular song *Happy Birthday to You*. Her presentation was in accordance with the Centers for Disease Control (CDC) guidelines. By March 15, 2020, my church closed, per the directive of the judicatory, due to the COVID-19 Global Pandemic. It was not long after that my wife and I suffered the virus that changed our lifestyle due to the death of my mother-in-law, who succumbed to the virus; my month-long hospitalization; and the virus making my wife sick and quarantined for several weeks at home. Nevertheless, the certified lay ministers *took the baton* and made a seamless transition, conducting the worship ministry and administering the church without any problems. Their performance of the ministry in my absence impressed the District Superintendent, Reverend Doctor Johnsie Cogman, Washington East District (WED), Baltimore-Washington Conference, The United Methodist Church.

To confront COVID-19, Mrs. DeFord, our son, Dante, and family members put into action the spiritual disciplines of fasting and prayer. Joining them were prayer teams from the church in conjunction with the wives of pastors. Their relentless petitioning of God proved to be effective; in fact, healthcare staff members contended my recovery was miraculous. In the meantime, Lila chronicled her experiences during my hospitalization and period of rehabilitation in a Baltimore, Maryland facility.

The Coronavirus infection not only caused collateral distress beyond the primary social relationships of the DeFord family, but also in secondary and tertiary relationships, such as among church members, clergy colleagues, friends, and various social organizations. Each person in these groups expressed their reactions to our circumstances.

We offer our reflections about the journey through the dark valley of COVID-19 and its impact upon our lives as servants of God. The raw truth is that pastoral families are not exempt from the hard and painful experiences that will challenge their faith. Yet, God is gracious and merciful to make a way in the adverse waterways of life.

Our hope is that our memoir will not be an ordinary tome but a blessing to readers and that each will know, despite this Goliathan pandemic, God gave, and continues to give, the necessary wisdom to slay this insidious giant of a plague.

Now, five years later, the world has moved on to address other circumstances, problems, and situations, such as ongoing climate change, famines, injustices of every sort, political upheavals, and wars. Yet, the echoes of the COVID-19 storm continue. America, with all its divisiveness, finds itself, through its national health agency, encouraging its citizenry to "get vaccinated" to protect themselves from the variant forms of the coronavirus. It is analogous to people cleaning up in the aftermath of a destructive storm, but many devastated victims, especially those who experienced the early onset of the virus, can still hear rumblings of thunder in the distance. Although a benefactor of God's healing mercies, ergo in my spirit, like storm victims, I, too, can still hear distant rumblings.

# CHAPTER 1

# JOURNEY THROUGH THE DARKEST VALLEY

"Even though I walk through the darkest valley"
(Psalm 23:4a)

Looking back, I liken our near-death experience of suffering through the Coronavirus (COVID-19) to what the writer of Psalm 23 describes as [journeying through] "the valley of the shadow of death" (Psalm 23:4a KJV).

My wife, Lila, and I began our journey through the darkest valley when my 97-year-old mother-in-law, Margaret McRae, suffered a stroke on April 6th and was subsequently hospitalized at the University of Maryland Charles Regional Medical Center in LaPlata, MD. Mother, who lived with us in Pomfret, MD, was also diagnosed with COVID-19. Shortly after Mother's admission, our dreadful experience began on April 7, 2020. We felt sick with the following symptoms: fatigue, fever, muscle aches, and shortness of breath. We drove to Right Time Urgent Care, Waldorf, Maryland, where the attending physician strongly advised us to seek medical treatment at a hospital. We returned home with intentions to go to the UM Charles Regional Medical Center the next morning.

Here, it is significant to note that Mrs. Almalita D. Robertson, church treasurer of Smith Chapel United Methodist Church, observed during the virtual worship on Sunday, April 5th, that as I preached, I appeared fatigued and not my typically effervescent, passionate preacher-self.

The visit to the University of Maryland Charles Regional Medical Center became a rude awakening about our sickly condition. For whatever reason, I delayed driving to the hospital until late morning, 11 a.m. Upon arrival at the hospital's parking lot, I was very weak; Lila walked to the makeshift admission tent at the entrance to the emergency area, where two women were attired in gowns, gloves, and masks over scrubs. The two staff members performed an initial interview protocol with my wife. After the completion of their interview with Lila, she told them I was too weak to walk. One of the ladies, rather petite in size relative to my tall, hefty stature, moving more like dead weight, brought a wheelchair to the car and miraculously and graciously assisted me in getting to the chair. At the admission tent, breathless and slow in speech, I gave the necessary information related to my age, home address, medical history, insurance providers, etc. Subsequently, I was wheeled into the emergency area, where Lila was already assigned to room 1. Later, nursing assistants placed me next door in room 2.

Attending staff members, also outfitted in protective garb, gloves, and masks, stretched over the standard scrubs and Crocs one is used to seeing, methodically affixed an intravenous apparatus in my forearm to draw blood, and an oxygen mask over my nose and mouth to help me breathe. Lying in that makeshift space separated by curtains, hearing staff quick-step back and forth in the hallway, it felt like hours had passed waiting for answers. *And how is Lila?* was the thought that repeated over and over in my mind. The nurses periodically checked on me and covered me with blankets. Finally, I overheard the emergency room physician inform my wife that she was positive for COVID-19, and he prescribed medications for her. Also, Lila was not sick enough to be admitted; therefore, she was eligible for discharge. The instructions the physician gave her included self-quarantine. After hearing what the doctor said to my wife, I felt optimistic that both of us would go home together since we had similar diagnoses. When the doctor came to my room, he informed me that I, too, was positive for COVID-19; as a result, admission was necessary. What a shock!

When my wife, Lila, left, I felt abandoned. It would be the beginning of our longest period of separation—45 harrowing days of helplessness and uncertainty—just as the world was uncertain about the total impact of this dreadful virus.

U.S. government agencies began reporting on the encroachment of the coronavirus at the beginning of 2020. The Centers for Disease Control and the Department of Public Health reported on February 29, 2020, the first death of an individual with laboratory confirmation of COVID-19 in the United States. The patient was a male in his 50s who was hospitalized with a strand of *pneumonia* with unknown causes and later died of his illness.[1] However, such news had yet to become mass knowledge among the American people, let alone the knowledge of preventive measures on how not to contract it—such as wearing face masks.

The Trump Administration declared a nationwide emergency on March 13, 2020, and issued an additional travel ban on non-US citizens traveling from 26 European countries due to COVID-19[2]. This marked the beginning of the COVID-19 Global Pandemic.

In view of my admission, while in the ER, despite my breathing challenges worsening, I was determined to muster up enough strength to make calls and to speak. I notified Rev. Dr. Johnsie Cogman, Washington East District Superintendent, the leadership of my church, and the organizations for which I served in capacities, including chairperson of program planning and spiritual leader. Dr. Cogman received the status of our worship program under the guidance of Min. Jocelyn Richardson. Mrs. Vera Littlejohn, Lay Leader of Smith Chapel UMC, agreed to alert the members of the church council of my circumstances. All this was important not only to let others know that I could not perform my normal tasks, but also to those folks with whom I may have come in contact. They needed to know of my condition.

Charles "Pete" Williams, chairperson of the Staff Parish Relations Committee (SPRC), got the news and called my cell. But his call came in just when the attending nurse charged with working to save my life was setting up my IV to allow meds and fluids into my body. Also, as I mentioned, bloodwork needed to be drawn. So, the nurse ended our call because she wanted my undivided attention. Pete and I spoke later in the evening. In addition, I was unable to contact Mrs. Denise Barnes, president of the Morgan State University Southern Maryland Alumni Chapter. Therefore, Ms. Joan Chapman, sister of Mrs. Barnes and finance secretary of the alumni chapter, served as my alternate contact to inform Mrs. Barnes of my situation.

Lastly, I left a voicemail message for Bro. Carlton Wourman, president of my fraternity, Zeta Chi Sigma of Phi Beta Sigma Fraternity Inc., to let him know that I would be unable to fulfill my responsibilities as chaplain due to my hospitalization. I initiated other telephone messages during what I thought would be my temporary stay in the hospital's bustling ER.

Depending upon the situation, I imagine most people headed for a hospital stay might innocently assume it's for a temporary timeframe. Yes, they may be pulled out of the assembly line of personal and professional assignments, so perhaps they confidently feel like a phone call here and a message sent there can serve as responsibility placeholders until they are back up and running on their feet. In the beginning, I felt no different.

\* \* \*

Data from the Chicago Department of Public Health reported in *The Chicago Tribune* on April 7, 2020, showed that despite being about 30 percent of the total population, Black people accounted for 68 percent of the COVID-19-related deaths in Chicago and were dying of COVID-19 at a rate nearly six times greater than that of White Chicagoans who accounted for about 33 percent of the population and approximately 14 percent of the deaths. These numbers illuminated for many the racial disparities of the overall COVID-19 Global Pandemic in the U.S.[3]. And it was traveling to my neck of the woods.

Significantly, with over 18,600 confirmed deaths and more than 500,000 confirmed cases in under four months, the U.S. was the country with the most reported COVID-19 cases and deaths, surpassing Italy and Spain as a global hot spot for the virus[4].

Another article offered (a glimpse) of the deadly virus's rampage in the U.S. "The first US COVID-19 death might have occurred in California on 6 February—three weeks before the first reported death in Washington state"[5] The article cited that the three people who died in Santa Clara County between 6 February and 6 March were confirmed as having died of COVID-19 per the county's Department of Public Health on 21 April. Also, the updated data included two people who died at home and a third whose location of death was not indicated.

The article provided additional information that showed the worldwide situation was grave. China submitted revised data that reflected an overall death toll of 4,600. On April 15, 2020, researchers at Johns Hopkins University in Baltimore, Maryland, reported that worldwide cases had surpassed two million, while the United States had 600,000 cases. MY WIFE, MY MOTHER-IN-LAW, AND I WERE IN THAT NUMBER!

"The death toll from the disease has also surged past 128,000 worldwide. Some 24,000 people have died in the United States, with more than 20,000 deaths in Italy. The pandemic has spread to almost every region of the globe, with only about a dozen of the World Health Organization's member[s] … not yet reporting cases"[6]. This was reported by Nature.com on April 15, 2020.

I wanted to make some other contacts, but due to the mounting stress of the moment, I could not remember phone numbers. Perhaps this was a prelude to the post-COVID era.

The emergency medical team prepared me for transfer to the newly formed quarantine section of the hospital for COVID-19 patients. I do not remember how long it was before the transfer; however, I did not see my wife from that point onward. Meanwhile, Dante, our son, picked up Lila at the curbside entrance of the emergency department and took her home. Our son returned and picked up my car, which was parked in the hospital's parking lot. Lila gives her account of our separation and her recovery from COVID-19 in Chapter Three.

The medical staff transported me to the secure quarantine area on the third floor—3 South. Once in the assigned room, a flurry of activity began: a recap of my name, date of birth, medical history, and current medications that I used. During the beginning days of my hospitalization, my severe breathing difficulties aside, I was weak but fully alert. The nursing team showered me with a lot of attention. One nurse connected a fresh round of intravenous equipment to me and ensured that the device functioned properly. At one point, an assistant nurse helped me to the restroom. Shortly after this, I became nauseous and needed to be changed. After being situated in the bed, a young African American doctor explained the status of my situation. She told me that my oxygen level was too low and needed to be consistent at a certain level. The staff placed an oxygen breathing apparatus on me and monitored my progress for several days. Meanwhile, a flurry of medications was being administered on a scheduled basis, and my vitals were routinely checked. I recall intravenous injections as part of the treatment regime. However, the oxygen readings were irregular and not consistently at the level required for a successful treatment. Eventually, my low oxygen rating would serve as a cause for my transfer to ICU.

Here began my fleeting memories of moments before my transfer to that ICU. I recall, while I was a patient in 3-South, one early evening, an announcement came upon the public address system. "Code Blue" was the message. I did not learn until my return home in May that my Mother-in-law, Margaret McRae, had transitioned on Friday, April 10, 2020, at 5 p.m. She was among the four patients who passed away during that week, as reported to the Maryland Open Portal Data, according to counties, listed under COVID-19 deaths in Charles County.

Also, I remember talking with Dante, our son, about unexpected contingencies, such as my possible transitioning while in the ICU. My main concern was Dante, promising that he would not put Lila in a nursing home in the future. Additionally, I informed him where our important papers were and who to contact should the necessity arise. Dante abruptly chided me by saying, "Rev, we are not talking about this; you are coming out of this place, well! We are going to pray about this." His opposition to this conversation led me to wonder, *My Lord! Was Dante listening when Lila and I were dragging him and his brother, as teenagers, into church for worship services?*

The attending African American physician informed me that I would have to be placed in the Intensive Care Unit (ICU) because of my low oxygen readings. Prior to going to the ICU on April 14th, another physician asked me a series of questions, such as "Do you want to be resuscitated?" The impact of that question caused me to become more anxious and fearful because my condition was that grave, although I spoke to Dante about unexpected contingencies. The last time I recalled such anxiety and fear was when an old friend of mine made a forced landing during dangerous weather conditions in a Piper Cherokee aircraft in a field near Lehighton, Pennsylvania, in 1973. I muttered a quick prayer to God for guidance. My response to the doctor was, "Yes."

Next, he asked, "Do you want to go on a ventilator?" The physician explained its function as a means of helping patients to breathe: a tube is inserted into the trachea and connected to a machine. To minimize the painfulness of the device in the trachea, patients are sedated. Also, the patients are carefully monitored by the ICU staff. I agreed to the procedure.

After my conversation with the physician, the medical team came to my room, placed me on a gurney, and rolled me to the ICU. I engaged in continued silent prayer—making this important decision without consulting my wife, Lila. Putting my trust in God, I believed that God's will would be done—no matter the outcome.

Looking back on all of 2020 until proven vaccinations became available, I marvel in hindsight at how there was a point—at which I found myself in the midst—when COVID-19 felt insurmountable. We watched as citizens of the world, the souls that the indiscriminate virus laid to rest.

The experience of being in the ICU can best be described as a blur and as being in a vivid dream state. I vaguely remember seeing personnel dressed in crisp white astronaut-like outfits: (what we now know as) personal protective equipment (PPE), white protective clothing with a connected breathing apparatus, face shields, and masks. It seemed to me that only the women attendants wore a different color headdress under the headgear. Perhaps it was a subconscious homage to the women saints in church, adorning beautiful hats. All members of the unit spoke kindly, uttering encouraging words to me. After being situated in the area, the team administered a sedative; shortly thereafter, I journeyed into a deep sleep. A member of the ICU medical team intubated me. The induced coma provided an opportunity for the ICU staff to treat me, especially during the extremely critical life-and-death situations that eventuated.

Oddly enough, there is a memory that sticks in my mind to this day. Post my intubation experience, during the early stages of my regained consciousness, I recall hospital staff members meticulously engaged in the procedures of the removal of a deceased patient from the ICU. In my clergy capacity, I have been privy to such procedures. I recall one of my late members being moved from the ICU to the morgue section of the hospital in that same white body pouch. Standing in the hallway as the staff passed me on the way to the elevators, the material shifted ever so lightly, allowing me to see her. And that's why the post-intubation memory sticks in my mind. In those moments, I also recall muttering (perhaps at a level that no one could hear but me), "If you need any help with funeral expenses, we [the church] can pay for it."

My treatment was fraught with complications, as I learned later. Lila summarized for me after my return home that my kidneys had failed, necessitating my being placed on a dialysis machine, and a blood clot formed in the ventilator tube, thereby requiring a new tube to be inserted in my trachea. It was a critical situation, and all the while, I was asleep, unaware, and felt no discomfort or pain.

The next time I woke up was on April 28th. Team members stood around my bed talking, but I could not understand what they said, and I could not speak. They seemed to be smiling and nodding in an encouraging manner. The next memory I have is a nurse leaning over my bed on the left side, rubbing my shoulder, and saying, "You are a miracle. We prayed for you." I did not comprehend the magnitude of her comment. However, I considered my pre-condition factors that militated against my survival, i.e., diabetes, hypertension, my age of 77 years, and obesity. The context of the nurse's comment became clear. Later that same day, a team member spoke with my wife and gave her the good news that I was awake and that I was hungry. Also, the staff member responsible for keeping families informed shared that the mortality rate for patients with the type of pre-conditions, similar to mine, and placed on ventilators was 80 percent. God was indeed gracious toward me with His healing mercies while I was in the shadows of death, my darkest valley. Thanks be to God.

A side-effect of being intubated was difficulty speaking. My throat felt irritated, and my speech was barely above a whisper, if not hoarse. I struggled at times to speak and be understood by the nurses. Dante pointed out to me as we reflected on the experience that my voice was indeed just above a whisper, and I seemed to be trying to learn to speak the language for the first time. For a preacher, not being able to speak is devastating. However, as time progressed, my voice grew stronger.

There are occasions when people mistake others for being someone known to them. My experience was during recuperation in 3 South, following my transfer from the ICU. An attending nurse with a mask and PPE, I mistakenly took to be a member of my church, Smith Chapel UMC. Her mannerisms and tone of speech were very much like Kimberly's (her nickname is Kim). As the nurse spoke, I was certain she was Kim. With my low, hoarse whisper-like voice because of having the ventilator tube in my trachea, I attempted to carry on a conversation, more like maundering, regarding her two sons. "How are the boys?" I inquired.

Her reply was, "They are doing fine."

During the conversation, I asked, "What is Gianni doing today?" The nurse responded, "Who is Gianni?"

I said, "Your youngest son … in high school."

She chuckled and said, "My youngest son is nine years old, and my oldest son is 30." It was perfectly clear at that point that *this Kim* was not Kimberly, a member of Smith Chapel UMC. *Nurse Kimberly* concluded our conversation by saying, "Mr. DeFord, I'm going to have to come by Smith Chapel, one Sunday." She patted my right arm and left the room.

In my mind, I thought that she really sounded like Kim at the church; obviously, I was in a state of delirium. I do not remember seeing or being in conversation with Nurse Kimberly again. In the meantime, efforts were in progress to transfer me to another medical facility.

I learned from Min. Rachel Stewart-Johnson, Certified Registered Nurse Anesthetist, Certified Lay Minister (CLM), and Church Superintendent at Smith Chapel United Methodist Church, informed me that LaTisha Williams, an environmental services employee and an evangelist in training while working in the ICU, prayed for the COVID-19 patients. I was one of the patients she prayed over. Minister Johnson informed LaTisha that I was her pastor.

In a cell phone conversation on July 21, 2020, Mrs. Hall recalled how she spoke to me during my time in ICU. She'd say, "I was talking to the patients like I knew them: 'Okay, DeFord, it is time to breathe on your own in the name of Jesus'. To everyone, I'd say, 'Oh yeah, Family! God is good! Miracles, Signs, and Wonders! You hear me! Mr. DeFord is awake and off the ventilator after a month! Hallelujah! God is so good.' Holy Spirit braced me for the good news before I saw [you]." She also shared how she became the weird, happy lady in my room. She was a natural cheerleader. She expressed to me how she could not wait to share it—the news of my leaving the ICU. Mrs. Hall informed her pastor, Bishop Farmer, of how I had come out of my coma and was now breathing on my own. The Bishop responded almost verbatim, with the same enthusiasm, as Mrs. Hall. Mrs. Hall was the first of the staff members on the main floor who cheered me on at my discharge from the hospital.

The next phase of my journey was rehabilitation. On May 8th, to my surprise, the hospital staff gave me a grand send-off. I did not want to leave the hospital with an unkempt appearance, so a nurse shaved the scruffy grey beard that grew while I was in ICU. Once shaved and dressed, two ambulance attendants assisted me getting onto the gurney to take me to the awaiting ambulance. With my personal belongings on the back of the gurney, the ambulance attendants rolled me to the elevator. I noticed a bit of excitement in the nurses' voices, but it was not until the doors of the elevator opened on the main floor that I saw crowds of staff members lining both sides of the hallway and in the lobby, clear to the outside. They were cheering me on with signs with such sayings as: *Brave. Congrats. We Crushed COVID-19. We Beat Corona. Whoop! Whoop!*

The greatest surprise of all was seeing Lila, Dante, and Robinette, my daughter-in-law. It was the first time I had seen them in more than a month. My wife gave me a big hug and kiss through her mask. I did not want to let her go! Inasmuch as the ambulance crew was not to be delayed, the ambulance attendants resumed rolling the gurney toward the exit, where more hospital staff lined both sides of a second hallway. Outside and at the curbside of the hospital entrance, the ambulance crew positioned me in the vehicle. I soon found out that local television news crews were on hand for my historic release from the hospital. It was also posted on social media. As the crew secured the stretcher and began to close the rear doors, I could see my family standing and waving goodbye.

Excursus

Here, I'm sharing segments of my University of Maryland Charles Regional Medical Center discharge summary covering April 8—May 8, 2020:

"Mr. DeFord is a 77-year-old male with past medical history … who was initially seen in an urgent care for cough and shortness of breath and found to have left lower lobe pneumonia. Patient was referred to the emergency department and was noted to be hypoxic and placed on nonrebreather mask. COVID-19 testing was positive. Patient was admitted and had a complicated prolonged hospital course as outlined below:

1. *Acute hypoxemic respiratory failure-secondary to bilateral viral pneumonia with COVID-19. Patient's clinical condition started to worsen, and he was transferred to the ICU where he was intubated and subsequently extubated. Currently patient is weaned off of 2 L of nasal cannula.*

2. *Severe sepsis secondary to bilateral viral pneumonia due to COVID-19—patient has been treated with a course of Zosyn as*

*well as hydroxychloroquine. Patient had developed acute kidney injury but has improved since. Patient hypoxemic respiratory failure has improved and currently saturating well on 2 L of nasal cannula. Currently patient does not have any shortness of breath or cough.*

3. *Acute kidney injury—patient was noted to have worsening renal function after admission ... Nephrology consultation was obtained and patient was recommended to undergo hemodialysis. He had associated metabolic acidosis as well. Currently renal function has improved, and creatine trended down to 1.3. Temporary dialysis catheter has been removed.*

4. *Dysphagia. After patient was extubated speech to evaluate was obtained. Patient was recommended to resume chopped diet and thin liquids without straw. Currently patient tolerating diet without difficulty.*

5. *Left pneumothorax—Patient had developed left pneumothorax while in the ICU intubated. He was noted to have clogged ET tube with thick mucus and suctioned was unable to be introduced. ET tube has been changed emergently. Chest x-ray was obtained that showed left pneumothorax and patient had a left chest tube placed with resolution of pneumothorax. Chest tube has been removed.*

6. *Acute metabolic encephalopathy—patient was noted to have altered mental status most likely secondary to severe sepsis and hypoxic respiratory failure. Currently patient is awake and alert oriented x2 but has occasional confusion. CT of brain was done that showed no acute changes but showed possible sinusitis and mastoiditis. Upon clinical examination patient does not complain of any symptom and no pain over the mastoid bilaterally. No sign of infection without any few or leukocytosis. Patient might need follow-up with an ENT when stable.*

"Patient is currently hemodynamically stable on 2 L of nasal cannula. He is awake and alert oriented x2. He is tolerating p.o. intake with chopped diet and thin liquids. PT and OT evaluated patient and recommended acute versus subacute rehab. Patient accepted subacute rehab and will be transferred this afternoon."

\* \* \*

The ambulance ride to the rehabilitation center was not comfortable, but it seemed like a short distance. I recognized some landmarks along the route. Apparently, I fell asleep because the Toyota dealership in Bowie, Maryland, was what I remembered last seeing until the signage bearing Loch Raven Community. I realized that we were in northeast Baltimore City in the vicinity of Morgan State University. Shortly afterward, the ambulance drove into the parking lot of the rehabilitation center, where the crew disembarked me. *Why have they sent me this far away?* I pondered.

The admission was quick, so it seemed. The ambulance crew rolled me to Room 23, bed 'B'. Another patient in bed 'A' was in distress as he moaned. Once off the gurney, a male staff member inventoried with me my personal belongings. After the inventory, the staff member assisted me to the restroom as I was too weak to walk. It was necessary for me to have a walker and a wheelchair. The reality hit me that I was completely dependent upon others to help me with routines normally carried on by myself—what a rude awakening. The significant issue for me was my loss of independence; I confess that reconciling the apostle Paul's advice to the Philippians to be content in any circumstance was difficult for me.

The first night in the rehabilitation center was not restful. My roommate, Michael, continued to moan throughout the night. Further, the nursing staff came to take our vitals and administer medications in the middle of the night. What became an annoyance for me was the nurses asking for my name and date of birth each time they came to administer the required medications.

Michael, the roommate, died one night during my first week at the rehabilitation center. The attending nurses, without explanation, changed me from that room to another room down the hall. I was in the new room for several days. I was just becoming adjusted to the new room environment when a nurse came and returned me to the previous room, which had been sanitized by the custodial employees.

My situation was paradoxical as I thought of the numerous occasions I had visited my members in nursing homes and how disgruntled some of them were; now, the shoe was on the other foot; I was a very weak patient needing assistance and upset with my condition. At this moment in time, I failed to realize what God had brought me through.

My stay at the rehabilitation center was not at all a pleasant experience from May 8—20, 2020. Although its mission is to rehabilitate patients to the best possible physical condition, attitudinally, I did not accept the fact of my weakness and inability to walk. Coupled with the reality that help was needed, I became angry with myself and displaced my anger toward the staff. Perhaps the staff viewed me as a grumpy old man? Moreover, my patient wristband indicated that I was a fall risk, so, of course, the staff appeared anxious about my falling. My sense of pride and dignity, evacuated from my spirit! I was not a good patient or a reflection of a servant of the Lord. *Have mercy, Lord!*

For the first week, my daily routine was sheer monotony. Being an early riser, I awoke between 5:30 and 6:30 a.m. and entertained myself by watching the news on a Baltimore television channel. Since there was no Bible in the room and I did not think to ask for one, my daily devotions were out of sorts, which added to my frustration. I yearned for my devotional reading materials that were part of my early morning ritual; as a result, silent prayers became my practice.

Initially, the meals prescribed for me were bland, soft diet, and tasteless foods. Later, toward the latter part of the first week, the doctor authorized a normal diet for me. Significantly, I lost the taste for coffee, which I typically drank at least three large cups per day at home. Certain meats, such as chicken, ham, and turkey, did not appeal to me. In fact, there was truly little that I cared to eat. However, what I did not understand was that I craved applesauce, ice chips, gelatin (Jell-O), and juice. Even now, we have a large supply of applesauce and gelatin with fruit in our pantry. My tray plate usually contained quite a bit of uneaten morsels of food when the employees from the nutrition department came to retrieve the trays. I lost a significant amount of weight, from 257 lbs. to 206 lbs., between my hospitalization and the time I spent in the rehabilitation center.

Key requirements were physical and occupational therapy, in addition to speech therapy. The physical therapist guided me through the practice of lifting two-pound weights and walking short distances in the room and hallway. My progress with lifting weights and walking rapidly improved. Eventually, I was able to walk from my room to the exercise area until, for some reason, the exercise area was closed. Nevertheless, I was strong enough to walk with the aid of a walker the entire length of the hallway.

I also noticed other physical signs. My hands trembled when I attempted to write; I was like an old person! My voice was still weak, and I tired very easily after talking. In fact, Dante, my son, felt that I strained to speak. My arms and legs appeared scaly due to dry skin. The lotion, in the patient kit, I used to rub my arms and legs, yet each day, it yielded the same result—dry, scaly skin. Both of my feet swelled to the point that I was unable to put on my loafers.

Each day seemed to drag on slowly and never ended. When the therapists came to work with me, time quickly elapsed; I welcomed their company. But still, I desperately wanted to go home to be with my family and in familiar surroundings where I could resume my normal rhythm of life. Nevertheless, with each day came the same physical routine: boredom, isolation, and loneliness were the emotional culprits in this daily routine.

I was able to break some of the boredom with telephone calls to family, friends, and members of the church. When my cellphone was low on its battery charge, the social worker, Mrs. Williams, allowed me to use her charger. Once there was a sufficient charge on my phone, I called Lila and had her contact my youngest brother, Terry, who is a deputy sheriff in Baltimore County, Maryland. Lila arranged for Terry to purchase a charger for me and deliver it to the rehabilitation center. The following day, my brother came to the center, where the staff did not permit him entrance and informed him of the quarantine policy. Nevertheless, the package with the phone charger was received and had to be quarantined for two days before it was given to me. Two days later, the social worker brought the charger to me, and I immediately began to power up my cellphone with the new charger.

From the time I received the phone charger, I called my wife and complained about my situation in the facility. Lila, in turn, gave me words of encouragement and prayed. However, my ongoing refrain to her was, "I want to get out of this place!"

Her reassuring wifely response was a gentle, "It won't be long, Rev."

The therapy sessions were beneficial. The speech therapist asked me my date of birth and what day it was, and then she gave me memory strategies for remembering certain things: write it down, repeat it out loud a couple of times, picture it in your mind, and make associations and relationships. The speech therapist gave me homework; I was to write about things of interest.

The occupational therapist helped me with routine tasks such as dressing, making my bed, and tending to personal things such as shaving. On the other hand, the physical therapist focused on strengthening my muscles so I could walk. In addition, the two-pound weights helped my arms. During a Saturday morning session, a physical therapist-in-training from one of the local universities worked with me. I could see my progress because of the daily therapy sessions.

My interaction with the night staff was problematic. The situation deteriorated and came to a climactic point. On a certain night, I called for assistance so that I could go to the restroom. After several attempts at calling, I recalled the technique practiced with the physical therapist of getting out of bed to use the walker. With resolved determination, I managed to get out of bed and go to the restroom. As I was coming out of the restroom, barely having time to be proud of my accomplishment, when the nurse, who happened to have a West African curl to her tongue, entered my room, yelling at me because I had gotten out of bed on my own.

"I have had enough!" I spoke back to her in my preacher's voice, "Don't you speak to me as if I'm a two-year-old!" Our blistering exchange was boisterous. I was certain it was heard by other staff members on the floor and at the nearby nurses' station. She watched me get back into my bed without her assistance before bolting out of the room. Not too long after, the supervisor walked past my room, and I called to him.

But he ignored me. Moreover, several of my calls to the nursing station went unanswered. *Do they care*, was my thought? The next night, I was assigned a male attendant. What a coincidence, I wondered, were they anticipating a replay of the prior night—and brought in muscle—the goon squad?

I recalled a comment from a noted theologian who said, "The biggest disease today is not leprosy or tuberculosis, but rather the feeling of being unwanted, uncared for, and deserted by everyone."[7]

The following morning, I told Lila about my experience and that "I want out of this hellish place as soon as possible," because I felt depersonalized and perceived as just another noisome patient. Later, Lila informed me that she and Dante planned to get me home by the first of the following week. "Lord, get me out of this place," I prayed.

It had occurred to me that perhaps the night nurse responded to me in the manner she did due to a recent incident in which another patient next door had fallen on his way to the restroom that adjoined our two rooms. The gentleman, an elderly White man, did not have a staff member nearby when he fell. His falling created a commotion because he hit his head on the door. I witnessed his serious injury because our adjoining bathroom door swung open into my room. Today, I note, it's funny about the things one remembers in these moments. Because I distinctly remember that he had a full head of silver hair.

And I recall a late member of mine from some years ago. She was a resident of a certain nursing home. She whispered to me, "Reverend, these night nurses I don't trust. You've got to watch them!" I attributed her comment to dementia. Well, now, I am inclined to concur with my late member, to some degree, considering my experience with that night nurse, although this is not taking into account my psychological state of depression, which was a contributory factor to my behavior. However, I confess that not all my experiences were negative.

There were cynosure moments in this seemingly dark valley situation. A very personable nurse's assistant came to my room each day with an effervescent disposition and smile. Her greeting to me was: "Hi, Mr. George! How are you today?" She was a pleasantly loquacious lady who spoke about her family and her husband of twenty years. At the end of her time with me, she always said, "Mr. George, you have a great day!" A young nurse from Nigeria was pleasantly quiet in her demeanor, each day when she routinely checked to see if I needed anything. I told her that I wanted ice chips. Shortly thereafter, the young nurse returned with a Styrofoam cup with ice. She wrote on the cup a Bible verse, such as John 3:16, and one day I wrote on a fresh cup, 1 John 4:4. These ladies brought with them the shining light of God's grace during my dark valley journey. In fact, they contributed to a sanative effect during my stay. I thank God for them.

Lila arranged with the administrative office for my discharge from the rehabilitation center for the following week, on Wednesday, May 20, 2020. Dante and Lila came to the center; however, they were unable to enter due to quarantine. A staff member wheeled me out and down the ramp to my awaiting family. My son attentively helped me into the car. The social worker advised that my Medicare insurance allowed me to stay an additional week, but that was flat-out rejected by us.

*Excursus*

The discharge from the Rehabilitation Center occurred as scheduled on May 20, 2020, at 11:00 a.m. The staff gave Lila my Discharge Instructions/After-Visit Summary—post-COVID-19. The said document presented the reason for my discharge with key precautionary measures and a description of the virus. The statement read:

"You had the COVID-19 virus. You were in the hospital because you were sick with a respiratory illness. You had breathing problems and/or pneumonia. Because you were improving, you were able to continue your care and recovery at the Rehabilitation Center.

You do not need any more care at the Rehabilitation Center and can get better safely in your own home.

- Make sure we have your phone numbers before you go home.
- Call first if you need to talk to your doctor.
- Talk to your doctor if you have any questions about COVID-19.
- You do not need to be seen by a doctor unless you have severe symptoms such as trouble breathing or chest pain.

You need to take special steps (see below) to make sure you do not spread the virus to others. You can spread the germ when they are on your hands or when you cough and sneeze.

The discharge report covers how the virus is spread, be alert to how one feels, seek medical help but call first, and the severe problems one might have from the virus. The said report stressed emergency warning signs and get medical help right away if any of the warning signs present themselves. The warning signs pointed out were:

- problems with breathing or catching your breath;
- pain or pressure in the chest that lasts for a while;
- not thinking clearly or hard to wake up;
- lips or face are pale or a bit blue.

The rehabilitation facility provided steps to be followed after the fever is gone:

- Stay home! The only reason you should leave home is to get medical care!
- Clean your hands and cover your coughs and sneezes:

  - Wash your hands often with soap. Do this for at least 20 seconds or use an alcohol-based hand sanitizer;
  - Do not touch your face, eyes, nose, and mouth;
  - Cover your mouth and nose with a tissue when you cough or sneeze:
    - Throw used tissues in a lined trashcan. Wash your hands right away;
    - Soap and water are the best option, especially if hands are visibly dirty;
    - Use a cloth face covering when it is hard to keep a social distance and/or there are many sick people in the community.
    - Wear a cloth face covering if you are coughing and need to be around other people;
    - If you cannot wear a face mask or cloth face covering, stay in a separate room. It is ok for others to be in your room if they wear a mask;
    - Put used masks and other dirty items in the trash with a trash bag liner. Wash your hands right away after you touch dirty items.
- Stay in touch with your doctor. Tell them you have COVID-19.
- Clean areas you touch often but at least daily.

- Stay away from people who are at elevated risk of getting extremely sick if they get this virus.
- Separate yourself from other people and animals in your home.
- Talk with your doctor if you have any concerns about how you feel.
- Do not use nebulized medicines or nose sprays like saline that might cause you to cough or sneeze, which can cause infected droplets to become small and spray into the air.

My discharge document described the virus as a new germ infecting many people all over the world. Furthermore, at the time of my discharge, it was hard to know everything about how it affected people. What soon became obvious (as time went on) was how most people seemed to experience mild cases while some became extremely sick and died. What was certain was that the virus caused an infection in breathing tubes and lungs. It readily spread on hands or when a person coughed or sneezed. The typical symptoms include fever, cough, and difficulty catching one's breath; the symptoms range from mild to severe. Those affected most were people over 65 years old; people with weak immune systems, and people with chronic illnesses such as diabetes, heart, lung, and kidney diseases. The acute problems arising from the virus are pneumonia in both lungs, various organs stop working, and death.

The discharge plan prepared exhibited my discharge on May 20, 2020, at 11:00 a.m. to my next of kin, Lila DeFord, with reference to psychological functioning and physical capabilities. The report indicated no cognitive impairment and/or mood symptoms. No home care was necessary. Hearing and vision were deemed adequate, and my speech was described as clear. Pertinent to household tasks such as meal prep, bill paying, and simple cleaning required no assistance. The therapy sessions, received during my stay, were physical and occupational therapies. Since I was a COVID-19 patient, the report indicated I should read the handout and use the guidelines at home.

Lila received the thick package of information from the social worker as we departed from the premises of the rehabilitation facility. In spite of my weak condition, I was happy.

My craving for a certain food happened during the journey home. What I craved was a one-pound broiled crab cake, one of the specialties of the Blue Dolphin Restaurant in Crofton, Maryland. Lila called the carry-out order via mobile. It took about an hour in traffic to arrive in Crofton, Maryland. Our crab-cake dinners were ready. The aroma of our dinners saturated the atmosphere of the car. I could not wait to get home so that I could delve into the food. The additional one-hour-plus ride home increased my appetite. Once at home, the food was microwaved; I was able to eat only half of the crab cake. I nibbled on the remaining crab cake for two days.

The next few weeks at home gave me the opportunity to become stronger in my walking, and I relied less on the walker and wheelchair that my mother-in-law used. Further, my appetite slowly increased. The taste for black coffee, however, did not return, although I began drinking coffee with hazelnut creamer. In addition, I began to enjoy tea with honey. Applesauce and flavored gels with fruit became regular menu items. Lila prepared familiar meals, especially with meats; moreover, the meats served were not like the translucent slices in the rehabilitation center. I felt content being at home and with my wife.

Lingering side effects continued since I was now a post-COVID-19 patient. I did not get out of bed quickly, as dizziness occurred and my legs gave way under me. I always made certain to have my cane nearby. The shaking of my hands began to subside, thereby allowing my penmanship to improve. My voice became stronger, although there was still some fatigue after talking for a while.

I had some problems with cognitive functions. My memory was not as keen as it used to be, in that I forgot words that I was about to speak; I referred to the problem in nautical terms: my drift rate was fast. I am not a stutterer, but there were occasions when it was difficult for me to say certain words or complete sentences. Lila noticed that I became *distant*—using her word—and I appeared to be staring out into space, or I had a vacuous expression on my face. Some refer to the situation as being in a brain fog. On a more recent occasion, I became very depressed because of a memory lapse, resulting in my breaking down into uncontrollable sobbing. Lila comforted me. During an afternoon Zoom Bible study discussion, my mind went blank, causing me to become angry with myself as I stuttered to get the words out. Honestly, I recall how, back in 2020, my memory lapses contributed to my reluctance, at times, to preach again ... O ye of little faith!

On June 3rd of that year, while I sat in the family room watching the evening news, suddenly, my heart started beating rapidly, and my breathing increased as if I were exercising. Lila took my pressure readings and gave me two baby aspirins. My heart rate declined to 49 and continued to drop. I remembered the experience of being with my good friend and fraternity brother, Dr. McKinney, when he transitioned; his numbers declined. I thought I was having a heart attack. My wife called 911 as I sat in the living room, where I waited for the emergency service to arrive. Then I became very nauseous, and the contents of my stomach emptied on the living room floor.

The volunteer emergency service ambulance arrived within five minutes. The ambulance crew, with their PPE equipment, came inside, evaluated my condition, notified the University of Maryland Regional Medical Center, and put me on a gurney. Inside the ambulance, I was connected to intravenous equipment while simultaneously being given a barf bag. The attendants also put two adhesive pads on my chest; I imagined, in case there was a need to use the "paddles" to shock my heart if it stopped. Another crew member joined while I was in the ambulance before it drove out of our driveway. The new crew member informed me that she was preparing a medication that would slow my heart rate, but the medication would feel as if someone were punching my chest. She administered the medication intravenously. In the meantime, a neighbor comforted Lila, who was distraught. Meanwhile, the emergency vehicle pulled out of the driveway with its emergency lights on and shortly thereafter turned on the siren while on the main road. I could feel the effect of the medication that slowed down my heart rate.

The ride to the hospital was short. At the entrance of the Emergency Room, two nurses met the ambulance. As the ambulance crew transferred me from their gurney to the ER's gurney, one of the nurses said, "Mr. George, are you back with us again?" I mumbled something, and she smiled and commented, "We'll take care of you."

My stay in the Emergency Room lasted from approximately 8 p.m. to 1:00 a.m. I went through a variety of tests, such as EKG, bloodwork, and X-ray. Chris, the male nurse, was attentive during my stay. He contacted Lila and gave her updates on my status. The ER physician checked me over. The doctor averred that once my results came back, he could let me know what the problem was. The room was cold, but Chris brought in enough blankets to keep me warm. After 12 a.m., the ER doctor informed me that my potassium and magnesium levels were low, which was the cause of my symptoms. I did not have a heart attack. My prescriptions needed to be changed, and I needed to be further evaluated by a cardiologist. I met with a cardiologist on the 23rd of June, who subsequently contacted me and relieved my anxiety that I did not suffer a heart attack and that I needed a change in heart medication. I now have the appropriate heart medication.

Lila and I met with our primary care physician, Dr. Peter Swaby, who was delighted to see us. Dr. Swaby went over our blood work reports, which were very encouraging because our A1C levels were low, and our other vitals were good. Most of all, our primary care physician was thrilled and relieved that we had survived COVID-19.

Another side effect began to emerge. I noticed horizontal dents on my fingernails on both hands. The dents seemed as if I had mashed both hands in a doorway. During a Zoom conference with my primary care physician, I was uncertain as to what caused the condition. The doctor stated that he would get back to me. Eventually, I learned that the condition is called *Beau nails*; the said condition results from extended illness, i.e., COVID-19.

After I returned home, my physical recuperation continued. I continued to gain weight, and my legs got stronger. Daily, I strove to walk in my community, where a couple of times, I walked for 51 minutes and 11 seconds without the assistance of my cane. My oxygen level increased to 97.48 percent while my temperature steadied at 98.06 degrees Fahrenheit. Meanwhile, my blood pressure reading was 113/70, and my heart rate was 56. I was doing better.

What a journey through a dark valley!

# CHAPTER 2

# MIRACLES, PRAYER, FASTING, AND HEALING

"He said to them, 'This kind can come out only
through prayer and fasting'"
(Mark 9:29)

Before full clarification of what this world could be up against, before the declaration of a global pandemic, and before the ability to combat it with vaccines, my wife Lila and I became sufferers of the Coronavirus in early April 2020. Uncertain as to our surviving the vicious staff virus, my wife's severity of infection was less acute than mine, resulting in her being sent home for self-quarantine while I was admitted for hospitalization. Our time of healing varied with her fourteen-day quarantine while I was hospitalized for a month, with a significant period in the Intensive Care Unit (ICU) of the University of Maryland Charles Regional Medical Center.

Considering my four-hundred-page medical report, documenting my patient experiences of hills and valleys while hospitalized, it is significant to note that, at that moment, there was only a 20 percent survival rate for patients of my age and medical precondition status—yet I survived.

I vaguely recalled a nurse saying to me, "You are a miracle." And while I do not recall the exact day, I heard those words because I was so sick, I can only marvel at their conviction. What a statement for a healthcare professional, operating from a framework of scientific training, to make. What did it take? What had she witnessed to cause her to place her faith in God and her belief in miraculous healing over and above her training? What made her risk the reputation of her scientific training to make such a bold statement? Moreover, I *had* heard the term "miracle" spoken more than once during my stay in the hospital. I was deemed a miracle; soon after the first one, another nurse said to me, "Mr. DeFord, you are a miracle." And there would be others.

In light of the ICU team members' reference toward me as being a miracle, the subject matter of miracles is beyond the scope of Lila's and my memoir, although some explanation is helpful to the reader to help him or her have an understanding of our biblical and theological perspective relative to recovery from COVID-19. So, what does the Holy Bible have to say or shed light on the concept of miracle(s)? And are miracles still operant in today's world?

There are mysteries in the Holy Bible that continue to mystify believers, non-believers, and scholars. The author, Herbert Lockyer, gives the description of the term *miracle* as the manifestation of supernatural power or the exercise of divine power. He cites Augustine's statement about miracles: "Miracles lead us to faith and are mainly wrought for the sake of unbelievers."[1] Moreover, miracles have a mysterious quality that can only be described as a supernatural working of the divine. Nevertheless, Lockyer asserts, "The biblical concept of a miracle is that of some extraordinary work of deity transcending the ordinary powers of nature and wrought in connection with the ends of revelation."[2]

The Old Testament (Hebrew Bible/OT) and New Testament (NT) use various terms to describe *miracles*. The OT uses the following terms: *oth*, meaning *sign*, and *mofet*, meaning *wonder*. There is a more frequent use of *oth* instead of *mofet*. Moreover, both terms are used in combination, for example: *signs and wonders* (Deuteronomy 13:1; 28:46; 34:11; Nehemiah 9:10; Jeremiah 32:20)[3].

The NT also employs such descriptive terms for the term *miracle* as *dynamis*, meaning *a mighty work* or a *deed of power*. Furthermore, the word *semeion* means *sign*, but when used in combination with *teras* (wonder), it means "signs and wonders" (Matthew 24:24; Mark 13:22; John 4:48)[4]. Hence, the terms relative to miracles in the OT and NT depict the nature of the mysterious, unexplainable action of a deity operating in the created order and/or human affairs to fulfill the gracious purpose and will of God in a given existential moment in time.

Miracles, as presented in the OT, occur pervasively in the created order as signs from heaven and earth, i.e., the sun, clouds, fire, rain, hail, thunder, and lightning. In addition, miracles are a means for meeting human needs such as food and water, healing, and petitions regarding life and death situations. Also, biblical characters figure prominently in the supernatural events, such as Moses, who appealed to God for deliverance of the Israelites from the pursuing army of Pharaoh (Exodus 14); the prophet Elijah who confronted King Ahab and the prophets of Baal and called upon God to send fire from heaven and triumphed over the Baal worshipers (1 Kings 18:17—40); and Hezekiah who pleaded with God to spare his life (2 Kings 20:1—11; 2 Chronicles 32:24—26; and Isaiah 38). In each case, the humans sought the Divine to intervene on their behalf to reverse and/or thwart the adverse and dangerous circumstances—miracles manifested.

The NT, the Gospels in particular, record a total of sixty-four miracles with twenty-nine of them healing accounts. The Gospel of Luke cites ten healing miracles. Typically, miracles are classified as independent units with the four Gospels. Notwithstanding, some hermeneutical viewpoints see miracles as historical events that happened in the past and occur now. Nevertheless, some interpreters believe miracles happened in the past but not now. On the contrary, the following comment written in the *New Interpreter's Bible: A Commentary in Twelve Volumes, Volume VIII*, expresses: "In this view, the factuality of biblical miracles is the foundation for believing that such miracles continue to happen. Contemporary claims to miraculous acts are in continuity with the biblical story. 'If God did it then, God can do it now …'"[5]. Brian H. Edwards, who wrote *Best Inspirational Quotes on Miracles*, says, "Miracles in both the Old Testament and New Testament had only one main purpose, and that was to reveal God."[6] Suffice it to say, this writer's conviction is that miracles still happen.

Prayer and fasting are spiritual disciplines that are part of the Christian tradition. As a Christian matures in his or her faith, the practice of prayer and fasting becomes a significant part of the integrality of the believer's spiritual formation. For example, United Methodist provisional elders who seek admission and continuance of full membership in an annual conference must respond to 19 historic questions, of which questions 2 and 16 ask: "2) Are you going on to perfection? 16) Will you recommend fasting or abstinence, both by precept and example?"[7] The ordinands are expected to respond in the affirmative as they strive for growth in their lives as Christians in addition to practicing and recommending spiritual disciplines such as fasting while not excluding the matter of prayer. So, it is out of the foregoing context that, as a retired United Methodist Elder in full membership of the Baltimore-Washington Conference of the United Methodist Church, Lila and I share our experiences as survivors of

COVID-19 during the spring of 2020. However, before sharing the depth of our experiences, I give excurses on prayer and fasting.

Prayer has many meanings, depending upon the circumstances. Prayer is an existential response to situation(s) that occur in one's life and entreats God for some form of intervention. A blessing, confessing, seeking daily needs, expressing thanks, seeking specific help, seeking guidance, protection, or requesting healing are the core issues of the human's verbal message with the Divine. It is a time of being honest and pouring out one's spirit—the essence of his or her concern—to the Creator, whether it is the good, the bad, or the ugly. John Chrysostom said: "Prayer is the light of the spirit, and the spirit, raised up to heaven by prayer, clings to God with the utmost tenderness. Like a child crying tearfully for its mother, craves the milk that God provides. Prayer also stands before God as an honored ambassador. It gives joy to the spirit, peace to the heart. I speak of prayer, not words. It is the longing for God, love too deep for words, a gift not given by humans, but by God's grace."[8]

Philip Yancy said, "… I see it is a time to keep company with God."[9] Keeping company with God is a relationship and a privileged opportunity to talk with God. Thus, prayer has multiple meanings but a single thrust, the human in connection with the Eternal Creator.

Herbert Lockyer wrote in his seminal book, *All the Prayers of the Bible,* described the various kinds of prayers in the Old Testament and New Testament; the publisher's foreword expressed, "Exclusive of the Psalms, which form a prayer-book … the Bible records no fewer than 650 definite prayers, of which no less than 450 have recorded answers."[10] Also among the many prayers is a thanksgiving prayer for recovery from illness and prolonged life, the narrative about Hezekiah's healing (Isaiah 38:10—20). Significantly, prayer was a factor in the ancient Israelite king's recovery.

Intercessory prayer is another type of prayer that is efficacious and powerful, as illustrated in the New Testament. In the Acts of the Apostles, there is the account of the apostle Peter's miraculous deliverance from prison by an angel and of the apostle going to the home of John Mark's mother, Mary. The church was in fervent prayer for the disciple while he was confined in the prison.

The writer describes in verses 5 through 11 Peter's confinement while bound with two chains and two guards in front of the cell door. An angel unexpectedly appeared as a bright light illuminated the cell. The angel awoke the apostle by tapping him on his side and gave the instructions: "Get up quickly, fasten your belt and put on your sandals, wrap your cloak around you and follow me." Both chains fell off the apostle's wrists. Following the heavenly being, they passed by the guards and came to the iron gate that opened of its own accord. The angel and Peter walked down a certain lane, and as unexpectedly as the angel appeared, he disappeared. The reality occurred to the disciple that he was not in a dream state, and he was spared Herod and the Jewish people.

The remainder of the account reveals Peter going to the home of Mary, the mother of John Mark, where there was utter excitement about his miraculous deliverance from the prison. Luke described that the house-church was in prayer when Peter knocked at the outer gate. Rhoda, who answered the knock, was stunned because it was Peter. In her excitement, she neglected to open the gate but ran and told others who did not believe. This was reminiscent of Mary Magdalene's report of Jesus' resurrection (John 20:18). Peter continued to knock until members of the household came and opened the door; the apostle described how the angel delivered him from the prison. Peter instructed the household to tell James, the brother of the Lord, and other believers. The apostle left for another unnamed place.

The narrative illustrates the power of intercessory prayer. The passage is a bookend, with the house-church at prayer while the disciple was in prison; notwithstanding his unexpected miraculous release from confinement, the congregants were in prayer. The members of the house-church in Mary's home were in fervent prayer for a specific reason: Peter's release from prison. This is reminiscent of the one hundred and twenty in the upper room in Jerusalem who prayed for power from on high, specifically the filling of the Holy Spirit (Acts 1:12—17).

The purpose-driven prayer is effective and powerful. As a personal experience, my healing from COVID-19 resulted from the efforts and professional skills of the ICU team members in addition to the intercessory prayers of many: the Intercessory Prayer Team of Smith Chapel UMC, The Prayer Warriors of Westphalia UMC, members of Asbury-Broadneck, Grace, Metropolitan, Saint Mark's—UMCs, Enon Baptist Church of Baltimore City and colleagues of the Baltimore-Washington Conference of the United Methodist Church. Some of the employees of the University of Maryland Charles Regional Medical Center prayed for me also. Countless others prayed for my healing. "Therefore ... pray for one another, so that you may be healed. The prayer of the righteous is powerful and effective," says James (James 5:16). Intercessory prayer is a key factor in the healing process.

Another factor contributes to the healing process. Fasting is the other aspect of spiritual discipline that is a contributory factor to healing. Jesus taught during His public ministry that fasting was integral in certain circumstances. The account of Jesus' disciples being unable to cure a boy suffering from epileptic seizures is an example of the necessity of fasting in conjunction with prayer. "But this kind does not come out except by prayer and fasting," demonstrates the importance of the two spiritual elements in certain healing situations (Matthew 17:21; Mark 9:29).

Fasting can be classified into separate groups and according to the purpose of the fast. The author, Elmer Towns, names nine fasts and describes their purposes. The Disciple's Fast is fasting for freedom from addiction (see Matt. 17:20, 21). The Ezra Fast is fasting to solve problems (see Ezra 8:21—23). The Samuel Fast is fasting to win people to Christ (see 1 Samuel. 7:1—8). The Elijah Fast is fasting to break crippling fears and other mental problems (see 1 Kings 19:2—18). The Widow's Fast is fasting to provide for the needy (1 Kings 17:12). The Saint Paul Fast is fasting for insight and decision-making (see Acts 9:9—19). The Daniel Fast is fasting for health and physical healing (see Daniel 1:12—20). The John the Baptist Fast is fasting for an influential testimony (see Matthew 3:4; Luke 1:15). The Esther Fast is fasting for protection from the evil one (see Esther 4:16).

Also, the author describes four kinds of fasting, e.g., normal, absolute, partial, and rotational.[11] The normal fast is the abstinence from food for a specific period of time. During the said fasting, one may drink only liquids such as water or juice. While, on the other hand, the absolute fast is the total abstinence from food and water; this type of fasting should be for a short duration. The partial fast is the kind that omits certain foods or is on a schedule that allows limited eating. For example, a person may omit one meal a day or eat only fresh vegetables for a few days. The Daniel fast is illustrative of that kind of fasting. Finally, there is the rotational fasting which consists of eating or omitting certain families of foods for certain periods.[12]

My wife, Lila, informed me how during my hospitalization, especially while I was in the ICU, she and two other spouses of pastors practiced the discipline of fasting for my healing. Mrs. Gwendolyn Kent, wife of the late Rev. Dr. Otto Kent, and Mrs. Stephanie West, wife of the Rev. Dr. Timothy West, fasted daily from 6 a.m. to 12 p.m.

utilizing the normal and/or absolute fasting disciplines. These ladies referred to themselves as the Prayer-Praise Warriors (PPW). Moreover, the PPW was a tremendous source of encouragement to my wife.

\* \* \*

A careful reader of the Bible discovers that in addition to fasting, there is a plethora of healing narratives in both the Old and New Testaments. Healing, according to the New Interpreter's Dictionary, is defined as "Healing refers to a restoration to health by any of a number of health care options, including but not limited to the body's capacity to self-heal, prayer and other forms of divine entreaty, and a range of biomedical interventions (e.g., the intercession of a gifted healer, care within the household, use of traditional medicaments, or employment of a professional physician)."[13]

The role of Yahweh is key in the healing narratives in the Old and New Testaments. Yahweh, as the understood source of healing, is the giver of life and restorer of renewed health. In the New Testament, Jesus serves as Yahweh's agent of healing and restoration of health. The account of Hezekiah's healing is a case in point of Yahweh being the source of the king's healing and prolonging of his life (2 Kings 20:1—11; 2 Chronicles 32:24—26; Isaiah 38).

The story of King Hezekiah and his healing from death is a unique account reported in several Old Testament books. Each narrative varies in length. Essentially, the king became aware of his imminent death as delivered by Isaiah the prophet. Hezekiah entreated the Lord, who recanted his decision to transition the king, granted him fifteen years, healed his illness, and showed him a miraculous sign of returning the shadow backward ten degrees. Each account concluded with the monarch healed with no judgment against him and the people of Jerusalem.

Jesus, in the Synoptic Gospels, resuscitated a twelve-year-old girl and healed the servant of a Roman officer (Mark 5:35—43; Matthew 8:5--13). In each case there was intervention of God in the human situation. Succinctly, Jesus resuscitated a young girl due to the plea of a bereft father. In the other account, Jesus healed the soldier's servant without being in the servant's presence.

The spiritual disciplines of fasting and prayer serve as a framework for understanding our perspective on healing from COVID-19 in conjunction with the professional expertise of the medical staff that treated our condition. In my estimation, this is why a medical professional, such as those nurses and others, could override their scientific training to look toward their faith to deem me a *miracle*.

The very cogent example of the house-church in the intercessory prayer of Acts 12:6—17 parallels the circumstances of the DeFord family during the spring of 2020. It ultimately proves that, despite the impossible odds of our recovery from a highly fatal and nasty staphylococcus virus, God continues to perform miracles of healing.

CHAPTER 3

# JOURNAL OF A PRAYING WIFE

"[T]hat you may be healed and rested. The heartfelt and
persistent prayer of the righteous man (believer) can
accomplish much (when put into action and made effective
by God ... It is dynamic and can have tremendous power)"
(James 5:16 Amplified Bible)

t has been five years since the incredible events of 2020! I confess, it
was extremely difficult for me to reread our first penning of *Miraculous*,
written fresh from our daunting fight to overcome COVID-19, and
my current notes of the experiences of that year. I experienced a mixture
of emotions: overwhelmed with a flood of grief, tears, pain, shock, deep
sadness, then joy, amazement, awe, and reverence for the power and
presence of God in our lives. I had to put the book down several times
for a couple of weeks before I could resume reading again. I simply was
not prepared for the avalanche of intense raw emotions that exploded
and overwhelmed me. I am grateful that Almighty God calmed and
comforted me. I feel my faith has continued to increase over the years,

as I have found comfort in the Holy Scriptures. I am frequently drawn to the psalms wherein I have memorized the following verses:

*"Come and listen all you who fear God; let me tell you what he has done for me. I cried out to him with my mouth; his praise was on my tongue. If I had cherished sin in my heart, the Lord would not have listened; but God has surely listened and heard my voice in prayer. Praise be to God, who has not rejected my prayer or withheld his love from me!" (Psalm 66:16-20).*

I marvel at the power of God and the ways He orders our steps!

The PPW Prayer Praise Warriors: First Lady Stephanie West and former First Lady Gwendolyn Kent continue to intercede in prayer and fasting for others. God has blessed us to have a new member, Johanna Coleman. She is a deeply religious young woman who is a committed servant of God! We are wholeheartedly seeking the favor of Christ Jesus in intercessory prayers for others. As I continue to reflect on the power and presence of Almighty God in our lives, I am comforted by the song *Trust In God* by *Elevation Worship*. The lines continually resonate in my soul, filling me with praise and worship for Almighty God!

"I sought the Lord and He heard and He answered. That's why I trust in God, my Savior, the one who will never fail."

My heart is grateful to our God who will never fail!

As a spiritual discipline and practice, over the years, I have kept a journal to record my events and prayers. My various Bibles and women's devotional materials contain notes and prayer concerns written in the margins. I even strive now, post-our COVID-19 experience, to keep daily accounts of events and prayer concerns. As such, I made daily accounts

40

of the circumstances leading to our COVID-19 diagnosis during the battle of illness and our recovery, as well as the many responses to what my husband, George, a/k/a Rev, and I had gone through. Looking back through my journal, I recognize that on many occasions, I violated a few rules of English grammar by using capitalization to emphasize my earnest emotions and reverence for Almighty God. Hopefully, the reader can vicariously feel my emotional pain during the toughest time of our lives. Here are my journal entries, softly edited—in real time:

**April 2, 2020, Thursday:**

Called 911 for Mother. Her speech is slurred, and she is hallucinating. Paramedics said they would take her to the hospital to be evaluated. I was dressed and ready to go with her, but much to my dismay, the paramedics would not allow me to accompany Mother because of restrictions about the coronavirus.

Prayer: *Blessed SAVIOR, please have mercy on Mother. You are the Great Physician. Please touch Mother and heal her, I pray. You know, LORD, all she has been through. (She fell on January 9th and had hip surgery on January 9th.) Please, LORD GOD, let your Healing Balm touch every part of Mother's body. Please guide doctors and nurses to do as You instruct them. Dear Jesus, Please help Mother, I pray.*

**April 3, 2020, Friday:**

Dr. Sein called and said Mother had a stroke.

Prayer: *Dear JESUS, my heart is overwhelmed with sorrow and worry for Mother. Please, JESUS, Heal Mother. My heart and soul are flooded with tears and pain within my soul. I'm crying out to You, JESUS, please, please heal Mother. She worked so hard during rehabilitation to get better and stronger. LORD GOD, please pour Your Healing Balm upon Mother, covering her from the crown of her head to the soles of her feet. Please, Merciful GOD, heal Mother.*

### April 6, 2020, Monday:

Mother was diagnosed with the virus.

Prayer: *ALMIGHTY GOD, I come before Your Throne of Grace for Your healing touch upon Mother. I can't see her. I can't comfort her, but I know You are with her. You promised never to leave or forsake us! A long time ago, Mother put her life in Your Hands and You, O' GOD, have sustained and kept her these 97 years. Please, LORD GOD, touch Mother with Your Healing Balm—let it flow from the crown of her head to the soles of her feet. HEAVENLY FATHER, please dispatch Your Mighty Warrior Angels to surround Mother, protecting her from all hurt, harm, and danger. Please, JESUS, help Mother. Please Heal Mother.*

I blacked out on Sunday morning and hit my head on the credenza. Rev called 911. I awoke with paramedics standing over me and a puddle of blood by my head. I was transported to the hospital, and a nurse put 13 staples to close the gash in my head.

My friends and former neighbors, Shelley and her husband, Jasper Long, left a gift bag with a dozen lemons, boxes of Cold-Eze, zinc lozenges, and two face masks. Shelley texted me, urging us to eat lemons and use all the lozenges. I sensed an earnest concern for our well-being. I think they were suspecting that we had the virus.

Prayer: *Please, LORD GOD, Bless them for their kindness, thoughtfulness, and love.*

\* \* \*

**April 7, 2020, Tuesday:**

Rev. and I went to Right Time Urgent Care in Waldorf, MD, to be tested for the Coronavirus around 8 p.m. and finally left at 11 p.m. They told Rev he needed to go to the hospital because of difficulty breathing. I did not want to go to the hospital because we had been there for hours while they ran a bunch of useless tests. I was so exasperated after being there for so long, and they did not test us for the virus, which was our purpose for going there. They said they needed a doctor's authorization to administer the test.

**April 8, 2020, Wednesday, 1ˢᵗ day in hospital:**

Wednesday morning, Rev was insistent that we go to the hospital because he was having so much difficulty breathing. He drove us to the hospital in LaPlata, MD, where a tent was set up outside of the emergency entrance. Only one person could approach the hospital staff person, sitting at the entrance of the tent. She was masked and gloved, and signs indicated we had to be masked to approach. When it was our turn (we were waiting in our car), Rev told me to go first. After obtaining information, the staff person okayed me to enter the hospital. When it was Rev's turn, I told a staff person that he was very weak; they got a wheelchair for him. We were taken to different rooms: I in room 1 and Rev in room 2, in the emergency area. After which, we did not see each other for a month!

After running many tests, I was told that evening, around 7 p.m., that I tested positive for the virus. I asked about Rev's diagnosis. I was told he was positive also and that he was being admitted. I was in shock. I was discharged to quarantine at home. I was given a prescription for medication, and my son, Dante, picked me up, and he had the prescription filled. And carried me home.

## April 8—16, 2020:

I have no clear recollection of what was happening during this time. I was so sick. All I remember is sleeping and only being awake for a few minutes. In those waking moments, I was praying for Mother, and Rev. Dante came each day to make sure I was taking my medicine and eating.

## April 10, 2020, Friday, 3ʳᵈ day in hospital:

The hospital called to say Mother passed at 5:15 p.m. LORD GOD have mercy.

Prayer: *LORD GOD, I am lost. The burden of this news has crushed me. How, LORD, can this be? Mother still had plans for things she wanted to do. Angel gifts she wanted to send out! JESUS, I can't stop the tears. I did not get a chance to see Mother to comfort her. LORD GOD, please have mercy on me. Please, JESUS, fill Mother's soul with Your Love. Please let Your Divine Presence surround and comfort her. My heart is broken. Please help me, Merciful SAVIOR.*

## April 16, 2020, Thursday, 9ᵗʰ day in hospital:

Prayer: *I thank You, LORD, for blessing me to become more alert. This is Rev's ninth day in the hospital. I thank you, O' GOD, for hearing our prayers for Rev. DeFord. I thank you, O' GOD, all through the night and day we are crying out to You, O' GOD, to pour Your healing balm upon Rev. DeFord. Praying You are breathing Your Divine Breath into his lungs, Ruach! Praying, O' GOD, Your healing hand is upon him. Please let Your Healing Balm of Gilead be poured upon Rev to flow from the crown of his head to the soles of his feet. Praying Rev. DeFord is being strengthened, healed, and cured of all sickness and disease within his body. Praying, ALMIGHTY GOD, dispatch Your Mighty Warrior Angels to shield and protect him. Praying You, O' GOD, are guiding doctors and technicians of health how to administer to Rev, according to Your perfect and Holy will. Please, ALMIGHTY GOD, raise Rev. DeFord up: healed, healthy, and well so that he can tell the world of the Blessed Miracle that You, O' GOD, have done in his life. In the Blessed Name of JESUS CHRIST.*

*Merciful SAVIOR, You have had us on an unbelievable journey! As Your HOLY SPIRIT guides me, I will try to capture all that is occurring because my mind is becoming clearer. We are praying fervently for Rev. DeFord. I thank You, HOLY SPIRIT, for Your comforting presence all through the night and day! I am constantly pleading with tears, heart-wrenching tears, for Your Healing Balm upon Rev. I thank You, O' GOD, for putting it into Dante's heart to pray and fast until You, O' GOD, have restored Rev—healthy and well to proclaim the Miraculous Blessings of Healing upon his life! You know, O' GOD, he's at death's door, but we know the Great I AM! We know the Blessed SAVIOR who has kept us and sustained us all these years! We are praying and praising the shed Blood of JESUS CHRIST over Rev's life.*

After not getting an update from the ICU representative by 3 p.m., I called. They said no change. ALMIGHTY GOD, I interpret that to mean Your Hand of Healing and Restoration is upon Rev. George DeFord. LORD GOD, we are claiming healing over George DeFord's life because You are the LAMB of GOD. You are CHRIST JESUS! You and only You have power over Rev's life!

**April 17, 2020, Thursday, 10th day in hospital:**

Prayer: *Dear JESUS, thank You for blessing and keeping us through the night. I pray, LORD GOD, for Your Mighty Hand of healing upon Rev. DeFord. The doctors are tapping into his artery today. They say his blood pressure is low. Please, Merciful SAVIOR, heal George DeFord. Please, LORD GOD. Please, LORD GOD, guide the doctors, nurses, and*

45

*technicians to do according to Your will and instructions to bring the healing that You have ordained for Rev. DeFord. Merciful SAVIOR, please, please, please heal George DeFord. My soul's overwhelmed with anxiety for Rev. I know, LORD, You love him, and you will not forsake him. Please, HOLY SPIRIT, let Rev feel Your Divine Hand upon him, restoring him, binding up and casting out every sickness, disease, and virus within his body. Please, LORD GOD, be merciful to George DeFord.*

*Please, LORD GOD, let Your comforting mercies be with the family as they go to the family viewing of Mother.*

I am still in shock. It can't be true. Mother is in Glory. I am still quarantined. I feel the lingering impact of the Coronavirus: hands shaking, weakness, and easily tired, and memory lapses.

Dante has set my phone up with the Zoom app. The ICU coordinator called and connected me through Zoom, so I could see Rev. He was in a glass-enclosed room that appeared to be 15' x 10', and the coordinator was standing outside of the room just holding the iPad so I could see into the room. Rev was so far away that all I could see was all kinds of equipment and tubes connected to him.

Prayer: *You, O' GOD, see him all hooked up to all kinds of equipment, but You, O' GOD, are the Great Physician. Please, Blessed SAVIOR, breathe healing and wholeness into Rev. Please cast out all sickness, virus, and disease within his body, I pray in the Blessed Name of CHRIST JESUS.*

**April 18, 2020, Saturday, 11th day in hospital:**

Mother's Homegoing Service is at 11 a.m. Merciful GOD, today I am struggling to view the virtual Homegoing Service. This just doesn't seem possible. I feel I can go into her room and greet her as we always do with the words from the Williams Brothers' song: "It's a new day and I'm still breathing, what a wonderful blessing I'm receiving. Thank God for a new day."

Prayer: *Please, JESUS, help me; there is a deep tear in my soul.*

The hospital staff called from the hospital this morning. They said Rev is resting comfortably, and they are beginning to give him nourishment through a feeding tube.

Prayer: *Thank you, LORD GOD, for this confirmation of what I already know, Your Hand of Healing is upon Rev. DeFord. You, O' GOD, are guiding doctors, nurses, and technicians of health to minister to Rev according to Your directions because You have made him; You are Creator. We are thankful for Your Gracious Hand upon us as we go through this dark valley of sickness and grief. Thank You, JESUS, for helping me to begin to focus on the things happening this month; it has been so confusing. Thank You, LORD GOD, I thank You for blessing my memory. I am remembering Your loving Grace and Mercy that have kept Rev and me. There are so many seen and unseen blessings we have not been aware of. I just fully realized that today is the 11th day Rev has been in the hospital. Eleven days, You, LORD JESUS, have been healing him and guiding doctors, nurses, and technicians of health to care for him as You, O' GOD, cast out the virus and sickness in his body. Thank You, LAMB OF GOD, for Your Blessed Hand of Healing upon us.*

**April 19, 2020, Sunday, 12th day in hospital:**

Prayer: *Dear JESUS, thank You for the gift of this new day and Your Hand of Healing upon Rev and me.*

I called in to listen to Smith Chapel's Sunday morning worship service. Dr. Petty played and sang a song, "I still have a Praise inside of me." Minister Taylor preached a wonderful sermon: *Natural Emotions.* At the end of the service, I came online and thanked everyone for their love and care for us. I asked them to continue to pray for Rev's healing. I thanked Dante [son], Robinette [daughter-in-love], Dre [son], and Lenora [his fiancée] for caring for me and Rev. I think the church family was happy to hear from me, as I was so happy to worship with them today!

Prayer: *Thank You, O' GOD, for the Smith Chapel Church Family. I pray, LORD GOD, You will protect and bless each member and their families.*

Dante told me he was praying and fasting from 6 a.m. to 3 p.m. each day for Rev's healing. I told him I would fast also, but he said, "No, I was still sick and too weak." I told Dante I would fast until noon each day.

Prayer: *I thank You, O' GOD, for sustaining me as I am fasting every day until noon for Rev's healing. I pray this small sacrifice will move Your heart, LORD JESUS, to heal Rev. DeFord of the virus. I am praying Dante's fast is blessing Rev, as You, LORD JESUS, see our sincere and fervent prayers for Rev's healing and restoration.*

**April 20, 2020, Monday, 13th day in hospital:**

Prayer: *Dear JESUS, thank you, LORD GOD, for the gift of a new day. Thank You, LORD, for keeping Your hand of Healing upon Rev. The ICU coordinator called to say Rev had blood in his mouth and was throwing up, so they had to stop the feeding. Blessed SAVIOR, Please, Please, keep Your Hand of Healing upon Rev. Please control and guide the doctors, nurses, technicians, and medical staff on what to do to care for Rev. For You are the Great Physician. You breathed life into him. Please, Merciful SAVIOR, heal Rev that he might stand before Your people and proclaim Your Healing Mercies and Miracle upon him. Please, LORD GOD, heal Rev. DeFord and all Your people who are sick and suffering. You, LORD GOD, have*

48

*enabled me to get so many things done today. I think I overdid it because I began feeling so sick. I felt the sickness was coming back, but You, LORD GOD, were merciful and calmed me and healed me. It was a great comfort to call in to Intercessory Prayer meeting this evening. We poured our hearts out to You, O' GOD, for so many individual concerns for Your healing mercies and guidance. We fervently prayed for Rev. DeFord's healing on this 13th day of Rev's hospitalization. We felt Your presence, LORD JESUS. You met us at Your Divine Throne of Grace—heard the heartfelt prayers from Your people. I was inspired and comforted by the outpouring of Your HOLY SPIRIT upon us.*

**April 21, 2020, Tuesday, 14ᵗʰ day in hospital:**
Prayer: *HEAVENLY FATHER, thank You for the gift of a new day! I thank You for Your Hand of Healing upon Rev. DeFord and me and your people who are suffering from this virus all over the world.*

ICU Coordinator, Karen, called to say the doctor would be calling me today because Rev's kidneys were failing. The ICU Doctor called to request permission to put in a tube for dialysis. The doctor said that patients Rev's age with the virus, 80 percent do not survive. The doctor said inserting tubes for dialysis put Rev at risk of puncturing a lung or rupturing an artery, which could cause bleeding. The doctor said I needed to think about what quality of life Rev would want. Would he want to be hooked up to life support equipment for the rest of his life?

Prayer: *I confess, LORD GOD, this conversation with the doctor shook me to my very core!! I was devastated! I could not accept this. I begged and pleaded to YOU, LAMB OF GOD, to have mercy on Rev and me. Praying YOUR BLESSED and HOLY WILL to restore Rev to a healthy, vigorous life. I pray it is Your will, LORD, because I know You have the Power to accomplish it! You have the Power to leave the doctors, nurses, and technicians of health amazed at what You can do for Rev. DeFord. May this be Your will for Rev. DeFord on this 14th day in the hospital. LORD GOD, I know healing Rev is a small thing for You to do with Your infinite Wisdom and Power. I pray it is Your Blessed Will to heal Rev, making him healthier than he has ever been. I look to You, LORD JESUS. No one can help us but You! No one can heal Rev. DeFord but You, JESUS! Please, ALMIGHTY GOD, have mercy on us. As I made a note in my daily planner, I was struck by the Scripture for today, "With God all things are possible." (Matthew 19:26) Yesterday's was, "... if you had faith even as small as a mustard seed ... Nothing would be impossible." (Matthew 17:20) Thank You, LORD GOD, for Your Blessed Assurance to hold on and to hold out until You, O' GOD, have Your say. Thank You, Blessed SAVIOR. Thank You, JESUS, for Dante. He is a great comfort and encourager to me. He did some household chores, vacuumed. He said we should have prayer together before he left. We got on our knees, and I prayed a tearful, pleading prayer for Your Healing Balm upon Rev. Thank You, O' GOD, for working in Dante's life!*

*I viewed the video, nephew Jock made of Mother's Home Going Service. It was a genuinely nice service, and Jock did an excellent job with the collage of pictures and music. I asked Dante to offer the video to Smith Chapel Church members who might want to see it. He said many members quickly responded to view the service and thanked him. Today was an exhausting day, but You, O' GOD, have been my strength, comfort, and sustainer.*

**April 22, 2020, Wednesday, 15th day in hospital:**

Prayer: *Dear JESUS, thank You for the gift of a brand-new day! LORD GOD, I am leaning and depending on You to Heal George DeFord!!*

ICU Coordinator Karen called; she said there was no change. Rev was critical. She said the doctor would be calling me today.

The ICU doctor called and said Rev had an exceedingly difficult night. They had taken him off the medication to insert tubing for dialysis. Rev was bleeding in the mouth, and a blood clot formed in the breathing tube. The doctor said it was an exceedingly difficult procedure, but they were able to remove the tube with the blood clot and put in a new tube. They were able to give him dialysis treatment. They have Rev on a blood thinner. They are recommending that if his heart stops, they would not perform chest compressions because of the damage it would do to the body. I just got on my knees and pleaded in the Blessed Name of CHRIST JESUS.

Prayer: *Please Heal Rev. DeFord!!! You, O' GOD, are his DOCTOR! Please instruct doctors, nurses, and technicians of health what to do and how to care for Rev. I pray!!! Merciful SAVIOR, please pour Your Healing Balm upon Rev, flowing from the crown of his head to the soles of his feet! Please, LORD GOD, Heal George DeFord!*

**April 23, 2020, Thursday, 16ᵗʰ day in hospital:**

Prayer: *BLESSED LORD, thank You for Your gift of this new day! I am grateful for Your covering over Rev and me through the night.*

Karen, the ICU coordinator, said there was no change in Rev. She said he was on dialysis last night and still on the respirator. She said Rev blinked his eyes, but they could not tell whether it was just a muscle reflex.

Prayer: *I am grateful to You, LORD, for this encouragement! LORD GOD, I give You Praise each time it is determined that Rev is no worse!!! The doctors, nurses, technicians, and anyone working on Rev do not know that Your Hand of Healing, ALMIGHTY GOD, is upon Rev. DeFord. You are casting out the virus, diseases, and any sickness within his body.*

The coordinator said she would call back within an hour so I could see Rev on Zoom. I thank You, LORD, for blessing me to be able to see Rev on Zoom today, even though I could not see Rev clearly because the coordinator could not go into the room, but showed him from a distance. They have Rev hooked up to so many things. My heart aches for him and all he is going through.

Prayer: *Thank You, IMMANUEL, for holding Rev close in Your Hand-of-healing and strengthening him moment by moment! LORD GOD, help me to Pray more fervently and continue to Fast for Rev's healing. I know, MERCIFUL GOD, You love us, and we are grateful for each precious blessing bestowed upon us—for each precious moment of life!*

I asked the coordinator about plasma treatment for COVID-19 patients. She said she did not think they did plasma treatments at Charles Regional, but she would check on it.

Prayer: *Thank you, Lord, for Dante coming every day to care for me.*

*Thank You, LORD, Mr. Gray came and mowed the lawn, and I was able to pay him for today and the last time he mowed, because when he came a few weeks ago, I was too weak to go to the door to pay even if I had the presence of mind to write out a check.*

*The Charles County Government Office called to inquire about our status. I told them Rev was in the hospital and that I was 85 percent healed.*

*I realized after talking to Dante and Dre about treatments for virus patients last night that I am a COVID-19 survivor! You, O' GOD, healed me of the Coronavirus!*

*The next time they call me, I will say I am healed of COVID-19 because You, O' GOD, have healed me!!! Thank You, Blessed SAVIOR, for Your Healing Grace and Mercy upon me!*

I received a cross in the mail from Rev. Dr. Johnsie Cogman, District Superintendent, Washington East District, Baltimore-Washington

Conference (WED), The United Methodist Church; I asked Dante to please text her to express my appreciation.

Prayer: *Thank you, LORD, for Gwendolyn Kent, who called me and prayed a powerful prayer for Rev's healing and mine. I was so touched that she reached out to me, knowing that her husband, the Rev. Otto Kent, who was a minister and colleague of Rev, died suddenly when hospitalized ten years ago. I pray, Merciful GOD, that You would pour Your Blessing upon Gwendolyn and her family.*

I called in and listened to Bible Study tonight. At the end, members were requesting prayer for family, friends, or self. I asked for prayer for Rev and my sister Gloria, suffering from Coronavirus. Audrey Chase prayed a powerful prayer for Rev's healing. Your anointing fell upon her! I was so moved after I hung up, I could not stop THANKING and PRAISING YOU, O' GOD! I could not stop PRAISING YOU, ALMIGHTY GOD, for Your Healing Hand upon Rev. Prayer is a Powerful Weapon, and my Spirit was overwhelmed communing with You, JESUS! I was walking from room to room, arms raised in praise-tears streaming down my face, shouting out Your Name: LAMB OF GOD, PRINCE OF PEACE, LORD OF LORDS, MESSIAH! I just could not stop PRAISING You, O' GOD! I am so grateful, BLESSED SAVIOR, for Your loving-kindness toward Rev and me! So grateful, I just cannot stop PRAISING Your HOLY NAME! Thank You, ALMIGHTY GOD! Thank You, PRINCE OF PEACE! You are worthy of ALL PRAISE!

**April 24, 2020, Friday, 17th day in hospital:**
Prayer: *BLESSED SAVIOR, all thanks and praise for this new day! I thank You, LORD, for Your Healing Balm upon Rev. LORD GOD each day they say, "No change," that says to me Your Hand of Healing is upon Rev casting out the sickness and virus in his body and healing his lungs,*

*kidneys, and strengthening his body to raise him up from this sickness to stand up healthy and well! Thank You, LORD, for the prayers that are coming before Your throne of Grace for Rev.*

The ICU coordinator called; she said no change. Rev is still on a ventilator and on dialysis. She said she had checked on plasma treatment and gave me information to call the Red Cross. She said she was touched that I wanted to do this for Rev.

Prayer: *LORD, please bless doctors, nurses, medical staff, and first responders for their commitment and hard work.*

Dre sent me a video of the Brooklyn Tabernacle Choir singing, "Hallelujah, Salvation and Glory to God". The video is such a powerful praise in song to glorify You, LORD. It inspired and comforted my soul.

The ICU physician, Dr. Young, called me to say that Rev was not any better. She wanted to know if I followed up, contacting the Red Cross about the plasma treatment. The doctor urged me to fill out the forms on the Red Cross website. She explained that if I were an eligible donor and if the treatment could not be done at Charles County Regional, she would arrange to have Rev transferred to wherever the plasma was being administered.

Prayer: *May Your Guiding Hand be with us as we pursue this treatment, yet my confidence remains in You, LORD JESUS! You do not need plasma to Heal Rev. You, O' GOD, can speak the Word and Rev will be healed!*

There are three friends in the medical field I contacted in the persons of: Shelley Long, Supervisory RN, Rachel Stewart-Johnson, RN, Certified Anesthetist, and Leslie Taylor, Medical Assistant. Whenever I am uncertain about medical practices and terminology, I call or text them. They always respond immediately with excellent information and encouragement.

Prayer: *LORD GOD, please Bless them.*

**April 25, 2020, Saturday, 18ᵗʰ day in hospital:**
Prayer: *Dear HEAVENLY FATHER, thank You for the gift of this new day! It is only through Your loving-kindness that we can Praise You and greet our loved ones. I thank and Praise, You Blessed SAVIOR, for Your Healing Balm covering Rev from the crown of his head to the soles of his feet, removing all sickness, virus, and disease in his body. Please, LORD, heal Rev with healthy lungs, kidneys, and a strong, healthy heart. Thank You, JESUS, for healing my head. I was able to remove the last scabs from the incision when I washed my hair today.*

*Thank You, LORD, for Dante and Robinette helping me take care of necessary paperwork (telephone, utility bills, etc.) and lovingly caring for me.*

*Dre, called. He and Lenora are making veggie bowls tomorrow and will bring them to me. Please, LORD GOD, Bless them for providing food for me.*

*ALMIGHTY GOD, I have every confidence Your Healing Balm is upon Rev. I am washing Rev's sleep apnea equipment today so it will be clean and ready when he comes home. I believe You, O' GOD, have Your Hand of Healing upon Rev.*

**April 26, 2020, Sunday, 19ᵗʰ day in hospital:**
Prayer: *Dear JESUS, thank You for the gift of this Sabbath day to worship. I was able to listen to Sunday School and worship services. You, LORD GOD, have so wonderfully Blessed this day for me. I was able to see Dante, Robinette, Dre, and Lenora! Dre and Lenora brought me a fantastic supply of food! Gracious LORD, I am so grateful for Dre and Lenora for faithfully providing food for me. They had come from Lusby, Maryland, an hour and a half away. They prepared two large shopping bags of a variety of veggie bowls. All I needed to do was heat them up in the microwave. They are trying to encourage me to eat because I'm losing weight. I wouldn't let*

*them come into the house because I didn't want them exposed to the virus. I just stood at the window and waved to them. I am so happy to see their faces. I am sad because I can't kiss and hug them. I thank You, LORD, that You have Blessed me to see them! Please give them traveling grace and mercy. Please, JESUS, Bless them for their loving kindness and care for me.*

*We are fervently praying for Rev's healing. Praying, LORD GOD, Your Healing Balm is covering every cell in Rev's body. Praying, You Blessed SAVIOR are strengthening his whole-body frame. Thank You, LORD GOD! Thank You, HOLY SPIRIT, for Your Calming Spirit comforting my soul.*

Gwendolyn Kent, former First Lady, and friend, texted me a beautiful prayer and message. She called me and was very encouraging and comforting. I told her Dante and I were fasting for Rev's healing. Gwen prayed for me before she hung up. About twenty minutes later, Gwen called me again. Gwen said that she and First Lady Stephanie West would join Dante and me this week in fasting and praying for a full healing and recovery for Rev. I was amazed at this—that they would be willing to fast until noon each day and pray for Rev's healing. Please Bless, LORD GOD, them for their sacrificial love. Gwen also suggested I Google 21 healing scriptures to pray as I fast.

**April 27, 2020, Monday, 20th day in hospital:**

Prayer: *Dear JESUS, I come before Your Throne of Grace this morning. I am reading 21 Healing Scriptures that Gwendolyn Kent had recommended. My goal and commitment are to read the entire list of Scriptures, bow and pray on bended knees, each hour from 6 a.m. until noon. Praying for Your Healing Balm to cover George DeFord, casting out all sickness, virus, and disease within his body. You have said in Your Word that some things can only be accomplished through prayer and fasting. Please, ALMIGHTY GOD, receive our prayers and fasting with favor, I pray. I was blessed by*

*Stephanie West's prayer that she texted at noon, the end of our fasting time today: "GOD, we ask that You make his bedside a cathedral for complete Healing. We love and trust You, GOD. Now have thine own way. In the matchless and Powerful Name of CHRIST JESUS!*

Gwen and Stephanie consistently text me at the conclusion of our time of fasting with words of encouragement. They are the faithful prayer warriors who have bonded with me—helping me to remain anchored to our SAVIOR!

Prayer: *LORD GOD, Please bless your servants who are willingly shedding light, love, and comfort to my grieving heart.*

Karen, the ICU Coordinator, called. She reported that Rev did okay over the weekend. She said he opened his eyes but was not responding to commands. LORD GOD, I am overwhelmed, You open Rev's eyes!!! The ICU doctor called; she thinks things are beginning to make a turn for the better. His eyes are open!!! The doctor said they are going to try to improve his breathing and order a chest X-ray ... he is still weak. JESUS, You are George DeFord's doctor. I am so overcome with this encouraging word from the doctor. Please bless doctors, nurses, medical staff, and first responders for their hard work. Dante's daily visit to check on me: bringing water, fruit, soup, getting mail from the mailbox, bringing up the trash can, etc. Dante was here when the ICU Doctor called. We were so happy! So, encouraged! My tears flowing! Dante suggested we pray to thank GOD. We kneeled and held hands, praying and thanking You, O' GOD, for hearing us as we poured out our souls to You to Heal George DeFord. We are so thankful and grateful, LORD, for we know it is only Your Gracious Hand of Healing upon Rev!!! The Smith Chapel's Monday Intercessory Prayer this evening was very encouraging. I shared my praise and thanks for the doctor's report today. Mildred Williams suggested that the Smith Chapel Church Family participate in fasting and praying for Rev. LORD GOD, I am so grateful for I know it is only Your Blessing, Grace, and Mercy that is upon Rev. Thank You BLESSED SAVIOR! Thank You!

**April 28, 2020, Tuesday, 21ˢᵗ day in the hospital:**

Prayer: *Dear JESUS, I come before Your throne of Grace, praying and fasting for George DeFord's healing. I thank You, O' GOD, for those that have joined Dante and me, Gwendolyn Kent, Stephanie West, Pete and Mildred Williams, and Vera Littlejohn. When Dante sent out the text inviting others to join us in fasting and praying for Rev, DS Cogman said she would join us also. I am grateful that these saints of Thine did not fail to step forth to give of themselves sacrificially to fast and pray for Rev. George DeFord.*

Karen, ICU Coordinator, called and said they are going to try to take Rev off the ventilator!!! LORD GOD, You have overwhelmed my soul with PRAISE and Shouts of Hallelujah!!! You, ALMIGHTY GOD, are Amazing that You would hear the prayers of a sinner such as I. I am so GRATEFUL Blessed SAVIOR! I am so THANKFUL!!!

Rev. Obie Wright called, and we had a lengthy conversation, and he closed with a deeply spiritual prayer for our continual healing. I am so grateful to Rev. Wright for his love and prayers. I am comforted and encouraged. I am anxiously waiting to get a call from the ICU doctor to report on Rev's status. It is now 6 p.m., and it is unlikely I will get a call from the doctor today.

Prayer: *I am praying, Blessed SAVIOR, please breathe Your DIVINE Breath into Rev. You, O' GOD, are Rev's doctor! Please, ALMIGHTY GOD, direct doctors, nurses, technicians, and anyone treating George De-Ford to do as You, O' GOD, instruct them. Please, GOD bless, strengthen, and guide doctors, nurses, medical staff, and first responders. Please LORD GOD heal George DeFord.*

**April 29, 2020, Wednesday, 22nd day in hospital:**

Prayer: *BLESSED SAVIOR, thank You for the gift of this new day filled with anticipation of what Great Things You will do in healing George DeFord!*

Karen, ICU Coordinator, called. She was excited! She said Rev was off the ventilator! (You, O' GOD, have breathed Your DIVINE Breath into George's lungs and healed his lungs!!!) She immediately hooked up to Zoom so I could see Rev. The nurse put the phone close to Rev's ear. I told him I loved him, and fasting and prayers are going up for his healing. I am so elated and filled with joy to see his face. I cannot remember all I was saying! Rev is very weak, and he has a long way to go. JESUS, Your Hand of Healing is strengthening Rev! So grateful! So overjoyed! So, overwhelmed with Praise to You, LORD GOD, for it is You that have touched Rev with Your Divine finger of Love!!! Called Dre and Dante. Dante texted the good news to the church family! I am so Thankful for Your Loving Kindness and Blessings upon Rev. This has been such an amazing day! Gwendolyn Kent called me and was rejoicing with me! She had to get First Lady Stephanie West on the phone. Mrs. West was driving and pulled over to the side of the road. We were so overjoyed with Praise and Hallelujah!

Prayer: *You, O' GOD, have poured Your Healing Balm upon Rev!!! LORD, this is a wonderful day of rejoicing and praise because of Your Healing Mercies upon George DeFord!!! THANK YOU, JESUS, I am so GRATEFUL! Please, LORD GOD, continue to dispatch Your Mighty Warrior Angels to watch over and protect Rev from all hurt, harm, and danger.*

I called into Westphalia UMC, Wednesday Midday Prayer-line. Rev. West said, "Struggles can draw us closer to GOD." Thank you, LORD, for drawing us closer to YOU! The hospital therapist called and said they were going to start working with Rev and wanted to know how mobile he was before getting sick. I explained he was very active: pastoring a church, swimming, driving, and golfing. My niece, Travia, called and prayed a beautiful spiritual prayer with me. In her prayer, she said even demons flee at the name of JESUS. Dante came and brought in the mail and a variety of snacks to encourage me to eat, because I lost about 25 pounds. I shared the good news! Dante and I got down on our knees and praying, praising and thanking You, LORD GOD, ALMIGHTY, for Your Healing Balm upon Rev!

Prayer: *Please, LORD, guide doctors, nurses, technicians of health, anyone treating George DeFord to do as You instruct them because You created him, and You are his doctor. Please, JESUS, continue to cover Rev with Your Healing Balm from the crown of his head to the souls of his feet. Thank You BLESSED SAVIOR for Your Divine Hand of Healing upon Rev!*

**April 30, 2020, Thursday, 23ʳᵈ day in hospital:**

Prayer: *Dear Jesus, Thank You for the opportunity to fast and pray for Rev. George DeFord. I am GRATEFUL that You, O' GOD, continue to pour Your Healing Balm upon him.*

ICU Coordinator Karen said Rev has been taken off the dialysis machine!!!

Prayer: *Praise Your HOLY NAME!!! Your Mighty Hand of Healing and Blessing have touched Rev. DeFord!!! I THANK and PRAISE You, LORD GOD!!! MERCIFUL SAVIOR, I am so GRATEFUL—so THANKFUL!!! You, LORD JESUS, Blessed Rev to come off the dialysis machine!!! THANK YOU, JESUS!!! I THANK and PRAISE You, ALMIGHTY GOD!!! Rev is off the ventilator!!! What a GREAT MIRACLE, YOU, JESUS, have bestowed upon Rev!!! My heart and soul are overflowing with Joy and Praise to You, BLESSED SAVIOR!!! Please, JESUS, continue to guide doctors, nurses, technicians, and all persons working with Rev to do as You, ALMIGHTY GOD, direct them.*

The coordinator informed that Rev did not pass the swallow test, so they put a tube in his nose that went into his stomach in order for him to receive nourishment. He also has a device in his nose for oxygen. Rev's voice is very weak from being on the ventilator. The physical therapist called and said they would be working with him.

Prayer: *I THANK and PRAISE YOU, LORD GOD!!! Rev is off the ventilator!!! Please continue to guide doctors, nurses, technicians, therapists, all persons working with Rev to do as You, ALMIGHTY GOD, direct them.*

ICU Coordinator Karen said she's going to set up a Zoom call with Rev tomorrow! I am so excited to see him! (I am going to have to do something to my hair and try to spruce myself up so he will be able to recognize me. I have not been concerned about my appearance.)

Prayer: *THANK YOU, JESUS. I am so Grateful for all the persons who are Fasting and Praying with me and Dante. I pray Your Blessings upon them for their sacrifice. Please bless the doctors, nurses, medical staff, and first responders for putting themselves in harm's way to help those in need.*

**May 1, 2020, Friday, 24ᵗʰ day in hospital:**

Prayer: *Dear SAVIOR, Thank You, LORD, for the 31 Healing Scriptures that start my prayer day. Thank You for the gift of this new day! I thank You, O' GOD, for those who have come alongside of Dante and me to fast and pray for Rev ... so grateful for the prayers that are being lifted up.*

I am so excited to see Rev's face and for him to be able to see me. (I have put on a little make-up and braided my hair, trying to look my best.) ICU Coordinator Karen called around 10 a.m. I was able to see Rev's face, and he could see me. I was overwhelmed with joy and praise. I kept telling him I love him, and Dante and I are fasting and praying for GOD'S Healing Balm upon him. I kept telling him I love him. The nurse in ICU was holding the iPad, so he could see me. The nurse said Rev said that he loves me. I did not hear him because his voice was so weak. I am so happy to see Rev's face. Thank you, LORD, for the Zoom technology.

Dante came around 10:30 a.m. and suggested we clean and sanitize the master bedroom in preparation for Rev coming home. Dante polished all the furniture. I sprayed area rugs with a carpet cleaner. Dante moved every piece of furniture so I could mop behind and underneath as I mopped the floors with Murphy's Oil Soap. Afterward, he put everything back in place. Dante wiped every conceivable surface with sanitizing-sterilizing wipes. He put the area rugs back in place and vacuumed them. I felt like I was going to faint a couple of times, but I kept drinking water. I am sure Dante was feeling just as bad because we are both fasting. Dante left at about 3:20 p.m. I am so exhausted, and I know he is, too.

Prayer: *LORD GOD, please give Dante traveling grace and mercy and strengthen him. I am so grateful for all he does for me! I am praying, ALMIGHTY GOD, You will Bless Dante! Please Bless him for he is a tremendous help, comfort and blessing to me!*

Mr. Brown called and said he had a gift for me. I put my mask on and opened the garage door. Mr. Brown and his wife, Wendy, were standing in the driveway with their mask on and handed me three framed tributes honoring Mother, titled "Thanks Today" (one for Rev and I, and one each for Dre and Dante) They also handed me two beautiful cards with wonderful notes of love and encouragement! They told me they had been praying for us, and his sister, Rev. Dr. Ruby Thomas, in Florida, was praying for our healing also.

Prayer: *Please, LORD, Bless them for their thoughtfulness, kindness, and love for Rev and me.*

**May 2, 2020, Saturday, 25ᵗʰ day in hospital:**

Prayer: *Blessed SAVIOR, Thank You for a restful night and the gift of this brand-new day! I thank You, JESUS, for blessing me to continue fasting and praying for Rev. Please, BLESSED SAVIOR, pour Your Healing Balm upon Rev, flowing from the crown of his head to the soles of his feet.*

Several persons called to check on Rev's status and let me know they are praying for us: DS Cogman, Rev. Smothers, Martha Higgs, Pat Mundell, Rev. Matthews, Rev. Tillet, his fraternity brother Willie Harrison, and Daniel Spicer. LORD GOD, I am praying for your continued outpouring of Your Healing Balm upon Rev. Please heal his throat so he will be able to swallow.

Prayer: *Thank You, LORD JESUS, for hearing our fervent prayers for Rev.*

**May 3, 2020, Sunday, 26ᵗʰ day in hospital:**

Prayer: *Dear JESUS, Thank You for this day of Worship and Praise. Thank You for keeping me as I am fasting and praying for Rev's healing. Please Bless Rev. Please, LORD GOD, Heal and strengthen his whole body.*

I called in and listened to the Sunday Morning Learning Session (Sunday School). Minister Rachel Johnson is doing a great job and more members are participating. Minister Jocelyn Richardson preached a wonderful sermon titled "Devoted". Dr. Petty sang, "He Touched Me", because of all the praise reports this week about Rev's Dr. Petty's closing song, "I found the Answer, I've Learned to Pray". The worship service blessed my soul. I was so lifted and encouraged. I know the LORD is working everything out, and His Hand of Healing is upon Rev.

**May 4, 2020, Monday, 27ᵗʰ day in hospital:**

Prayer: *Dear JESUS, Thank You for Your Blessings upon Dante and me , Prayer Warriors, Ms. Gwen and Mrs. West as we continue to fast and pray for Rev. DeFord's healing. Thank You, O' GOD, for those who have joined us: Vera Littlejohn, Mildres and Charles Williams, in fasting and praying. Merciful GOD, You are Rev's doctor. Please heal every bone, muscle, and cell in his body. Please guide the doctors, nurses, technicians, therapists, and anyone who works with Rev.*

There have been several calls today, but I am determined to stick to the schedule of reading 31 Healing Scriptures and praying each hour on bended knees. I began calling the hospital to get an update on Rev, but the nurse did not answer the page. I called the hospital again and left a message.

Dante came and brought up mail and carried the trash can down. He brought me some groceries, some plug-in fragrances, and several swifter dust items. He also sprayed repellent on the porch. Thank you, Jesus, for all Dante does to care for me. Please, LORD bless him, I pray.

I thank You, Blessed SAVIOR, Nurse Jessica returned my call. She said Rev has been very alert today, and he told her he is hungry! LORD GOD, this is an Amazing Blessing directly from You, You! ALMIGHTY GOD to me!! LORD GOD, You are assuring me of Your Divine Hand of Healing upon Rev, touching his body so he can feel hunger! LORD, You know Rev has an appetite! Thank You JESUS!! Rev is hungry!! LORD GOD, You are Healing Rev! Hallelujah!!! Praise Your HOLY NAME! All I can say is THANK YOU! THANK YOU! THANK YOU! THANK YOU! PRAISE YOU! JESUS!!

Nurse Jessica said she gave Rev pudding. She said that she was waiting for the speech therapist to evaluate Rev because they do not want him to aspirate. The nurse says he is moving a little bit, but he is very weak. Thank You, JESUS! I am rejoicing, I am ecstatic, for this Wonderful Blessing upon Rev!!

**May 5, 2020, Tuesday, 28ᵗʰ day in hospital:**

Prayer: *Blessed SAVIOR, I greet You this day with a joyful heart! Thank You for the wonderful Blessings upon Rev. You, O' GOD, have touched him with Your finger of love. I am coming before Your throne of grace, fasting and praying for Rev's complete healing.*

I spoke to Nurse Jessica. She said that Rev was feeding himself. They are giving him chopped food, which is a step above puréed. I asked if there was a phone in his room. The nurse said, "Yes," and gave me the phone number. I called, and the nurse handed Rev the phone. I talked to him for about 5-7 minutes, telling him I love him and miss him. I told him how the church was doing such a wonderful job keeping the ministries going. He said that God had him in the right place. I asked how he was feeling, and he said that his back hurt. I told him he's been in the hospital for 27 days. He said that he wanted to know about Mother's funeral. I purposely had not mentioned it because I didn't know if he knew Mother had passed. Just then, the nurse asked me if I would like to see Rev having physical therapy. She said they would call me when the therapy session began. The case manager, Lori Parson, called and said Rev would be ready to transfer to a rehabilitation facility this week. She emailed me a list of facilities that would take COVID-19 patients. This was wonderful news and disturbing at the same time. I thought the treatment would be at the hospital, and he would come home from there. I prayed, "LORD GOD, please guide me! Please tell me what to do!"

Karen, the ICU Coordinator, was getting set up on Zoom. She said that Rev is a Miracle! She gave the iPad to the nurse and introduced me to the physical therapists. The nurse positioned the iPad so I could see the "PT" session today. Rev was able to raise his legs, bend his arms back and forth. The staff and I were cheering him on! The therapist tried to get him to stand with their assistance, supporting him, but he was only able to stand for 2-3 seconds. He was so exhausted. They got him situated back in the bed.

Prayer: *I thank You, LORD, for letting me see that Rev does need rehabilitation to regain his strength.*

I called my friend, Shelley, RN, for assistance in selecting a rehabilitation facility. She recommended the National Rehabilitation Hospital (NRH).

This evening, DS Cogman called asking me for a confirmation statement indicating Rev's request for retirement from pastoring at Smith Chapel United Methodist Church, effective July 1, 2020. DS Cogman said that she needed this information ASAP. This placed such a heavy weight upon me. I will discuss the matter with Rev tomorrow.

Prayer: *LORD GOD, please help me to have this conversation with Rev. His health is so fragile. Serving as an under-shepherd to your people has been the greatest joy of his life. LORD GOD, it breaks my heart to have this talk with Rev. His whole life is wrapped up in serving in ministry to proclaim the good news of JESUS CHRIST.*

*Merciful GOD, it is Your Love that has covered me through each difficult decision and heart-breaking moment of this journey. More than that, ALMIGHTY GOD, You have held us in the palm of Your Hand … reassuring us of Your love, grace, and mercy.*

### May 6, 2020, Wednesday, 29th day in hospital:

Prayer: *Dear JESUS, thank You for the gift of the new day. Thank You for blessing this time of fasting and praying for Rev's healing. Please bless those who are praying and fasting with Dante and me.*

Case manager, Lori Parsons, called; she is pressing me to make a decision on which rehabilitation facility I've selected. I told her that

I selected National Rehabilitation Hospital, NRH, in Washington, DC. Although it was not on her list, I would like Rev to go there for physical therapy. Ms. Parson indicated that she would call and get back in touch with me. The case manager called back later and informed me that NRH does take COVID-19 patients but would not accept Rev because he would need to be able to do four hours of physical therapy a day. Ms. Parsons says she's meeting with the doctor, and she needs my decision for a rehab facility. She still has not given me a specific date when Rev will be discharged.

Dante came with a man who pulled weeds in the flower beds and trimmed the hedges. He did an incredibly excellent job. Dante put flowers in all my pots on the front porch. Everything looks beautiful. Thank You, JESUS, for Dante. Please ALMIGHTY GOD bless Dante for all he does for me. I am so grateful for his loving care.

I talked with Rev this afternoon about my conversation with DS Cogman. He said it was okay to tell her he was retiring as pastor of Smith Chapel UMC, effective July 1, 2020. I know this is a heartbreaking decision for Rev. George DeFord. He has always considered it a great honor and privilege that You, Blessed SAVIOR, called him to serve Your people. Rev's whole life has been wrapped up in being the under-Shepherd to serve You. How I wish I could be with Rev today, to hold his hands and pray. My heart aches for Rev making this tough decision. I can't hold back the tears. Rev has been a faithful, committed servant for over 40 years and is now stepping down. With his present health situation, he's concerned that the members should have a pastor who is healthy and well to lead them. I texted DS Cogman about Rev's decision. She immediately called me to confirm my text. She said she was going to call Mr. Charles Williams, Chair, Staff Parish Relations Committee, to begin the process for a new pastor of Smith Chapel.

I called Rev later this evening. He's very concerned about his physical limitations and rehab. I told him he can do it. He's concerned about whether he will be able to drive. I assured him that he will. I tried to be positive and kept reassuring him. Apparently, it was working because the conversation shifted to Rev's craving for his favorite foods. He wanted Dante to get crab cakes from his favorite restaurant, and Dre to get a lemon meringue pie that he liked from Wegmans.

Prayer: *LORD GOD, please keep him thinking about positive things. Thank You, DEAR JESUS, for blessings seen and unseen. Thank You for being my refuge. Thank You for sustaining me as I have been leaning my whole weight upon You. LAMB OF GOD, thank You for Your Healing Balm upon Rev. Please continue to strengthen every fiber of his being. Please heal his whole-body frame so that he will be able to stand and walk. Thank You, LORD, for Your loving-kindness, grace, and mercy upon us.*

### May 7, 2020, Thursday, 30th day in hospital:

Prayer: *DEAR JESUS, Praising and thankful for the gift of this new day. Praying and fasting for Rev's healing. Please pour Your Healing Balm upon Rev. Please let it flow from the crown of his head to the soles of his feet. Please strengthen his whole-body frame. Please heal his throat, lungs, bones, and muscles. You, O' GOD, are Rev's doctor!*

Lori, the case manager, called to say that the rehabilitation facility in Baltimore, Maryland, is ready to admit Rev today. I asked if they had talked to Rev. She said she doesn't go on the floor, so she didn't know. Further, she said Rev was tested yesterday and he's still positive for Coronavirus. The case manager said she was having a conference call with the doctors and would call me after 2 p.m. With their recommendation. Lori called me back and said that the doctor says Rev is medically ready to be discharged from the hospital, but physically not able to go home. They are recommending transferring him to a rehab facility. The said facility is ready to receive Rev now.

I asked them to delay the discharge until tomorrow so I could talk to my husband about the transfer. I called Rev. He had difficulty manipulating the phone, kept pushing the wrong buttons, so Dante and I kept getting a busy signal. I had to call the nurses to ask if they would help him with the phone. I told Rev he would be discharged from the hospital and transferred to a rehabilitation facility tomorrow. I'm very disturbed that the only rehab facility available for Rev did not have favorable reviews. I am overly concerned because this is a rehab and nursing home. I wanted Rev in a facility exclusively for rehabilitation. I can't stop crying—very emotional today.

One of the staff called this evening and said they found another facility that was rehab-only, the University of Maryland Rehab Center, but Rev would have to be negative for the virus. So, they are re-testing Rev for the virus. She assured me they were not giving up. They weren't giving up because they wanted to comply with my request to get Rev in a strictly rehab facility, not the combined rehab/nursing home facility. They said they had called NRH again, urging them to please make an exception and accept Rev. Also, she was working on celebrating Rev's leaving the hospital tomorrow. She asked if it would be okay to take pictures. She said they asked Rev, and he said, "Okay." However, they wanted my approval, also. I agreed and was told I would need to sign consent papers tomorrow.

I called Gwen and asked her to pray for the better facility to be available for Rev. We had a long chat. She was very comforting and encouraging. Gwen closed our conversation with prayer:

"Whatever rehab place Rev goes to, the standards would be raised to GOD's level. GOD will provide the best care for Rev!" Thank YOU, BLESSED SAVIOR, for this faithful Prayer Praise Warrior.

## May 8, 2020, 30<sup>th</sup> day in hospital:

Prayer: *Dear HEAVENLY FATHER, thank You, Merciful SAVIOR, for the gift of this new day. Thank You, LORD, for Your Healing Balm upon Rev.*

Today, Rev will be discharged from the hospital and transported to a rehab facility. I am so overjoyed, LORD GOD, that Your Hand of Healing raised Rev up! The case manager called to say Rev failed the COVID-19 test, so he would not be accepted at the University of Maryland Rehab Center. I am extremely disappointed. I was praying that Rev would be able to go to a better facility. As I was fasting and praying, I felt Your comforting assurance that You, LORD GOD, have everything under control—to trust You. I was not going to let this discourage me! Today, I am going to see George DeFord!!!

I began sprucing myself up. I'm so excited that I will have the opportunity to see Rev!! I have not seen him for a whole month, and I'll only be able to see him for 2-3 minutes before he's placed in the ambulance transporting him to the rehab facility. COVID restrictions will not permit me to see him in the rehab center.

Lori said the staff would get in contact with me about the arrangements. Since I didn't know what time the hospital would call with the information, Dante and Robinette arranged to pick me up and carry me to their house, which is five minutes away from the hospital. I'm so fidgety waiting for the hospital to call. This is the first time I've been out since getting sick, and the first time I'm wearing something other than a robe and slippers. I've suddenly realized I lost 25-30 pounds during this time because my clothes are feeling too big. I needed a safety pin for my pants. Finally, we got instructions: the time and which entrance of the hospital to come to. We were told only two persons would be permitted. Robinette sadly agreed to stay at home. When Dante and

I entered the hospital, we were shocked to see the whole hospital staff lined up on both sides of the corridor. Lori met us at the entrance and directed us to a place to stand. I'm amazed as I looked around at the signs and posters the staff were holding: "We Beat Corona! We Crush COVID-19! Congrats! Home of the Brave!" I was told there was an issue about the time the ambulance would arrive; instead of 35-45 minutes, it would be two hours later. Chairs were brought for us to sit, but I couldn't sit down, I was too excited and so anxious to see Rev!!!

As we waited, different staff members came over and introduced themselves to tell me what treatment they had done for Rev. I met ICU Dr. Young, a physician who put in his ventilator tube; Karen, the ICU Coordinator; and the physical therapists. Several staff members took pictures with me. Our friend Rachel Johnson suggested we should call Robinette to come join us at the hospital. She was so happy and got to the hospital in less than five minutes. I kept looking towards the entrance for the ambulance to arrive. Finally, the ambulance pulled up. The ambulance crew brought the stretcher in and got on the elevator to the floor where Rev's room was located. It was 35-45 minutes before they got off the elevator, rolling Rev out! I was so overjoyed! The hospital staff began cheering, clapping, and waving signs. As the stretcher neared me, I stepped from the sidelines. I hugged and kissed him, telling him I love you. Rev hugged me tight. Dante and Robinette hugged him. I hugged him again, so overwhelmed with tears of joy. The ambulance crew proceeded to the ambulance to transport him to the rehab center. I shall never forget those brief moments!

Prayer: *Thank You, ALMIGHTY GOD, for this miracle!!! You have raised Rev from the doorway of death to wellness and life!!! My soul is overjoyed, I am so amazed!! I can hardly comprehend the Awesomeness of this Blessing!! Thank You, LORD, for hearing and answering our fervent prayers for Rev. Truly, I am the least of thy servants, and yet You loved me to life—You Loved Rev to life! I am so Grateful! So Thankful! It's all because of You, JESUS! You restored Rev to life! You ALMIGHTY GOD gave us the Precious Gift of Life! BLESSED SAVIOR, my soul is rejoicing with THANKS and PRAISE for I know You Redeemed George DeFord! I Glorify Your HOLY NAME!*

We had planned to take pictures of this precious moment, but we were so caught up in the moment, we forgot. Thankfully, the hospital staff not only took pictures but also a video. By 6:30 this evening, they sent the pictures and video to us. Thank You, JESUS, we have these pictures and video that we can look at over and over! Dante immediately sent the video to church members, and family, and friends so they could share in this precious moment of Your Miraculous Blessings upon us. ALL the Praise belongs to You, LORD GOD, ALMIGHTY!!!

**May 9, 2020, Saturday, 2ⁿᵈ day in Rehabilitation Facility:**

Prayer: *Dear Jesus, Thank You for the gift of this new day! My soul is still rejoicing that I was able to see and hug Rev yesterday! LORD GOD, Thank You for Your Miraculous Hand of Healing upon George DeFord! I am so Grateful that Rev is alive! It was You, LORD, that raised Rev up from this severe sickness! It was You, LORD, who breathed into his lungs! It was You, LORD, who started his kidneys functioning! It was Your Divine Hand of Love that touched Rev! Merciful GOD, I PRAISE YOU! I WORSHIP You! I Glorify Your HOLY NAME!*

Last evening, Rev was taken by ambulance to the rehabilitation center in Baltimore, Maryland. I had hoped Rev would be coming home from the hospital, but I complied with the doctor's orders for rehabilitation. Dante, I, and Prayer Praise Warriors continue to fast and pray for Rev's complete healing. We are so appreciative of our

Church family, friends, and everyone who is praying for us. I talked to Rev. He wanted to know why he's in Baltimore. He remembered the ambulance passing near Morgan State University. I explained that this was the only rehabilitation facility available, taking Coronavirus patients. I assured him I was still in contact with Lori Parsons at Charles Regional Hospital, trying to arrange to have him transferred to another facility. Please help me, LORD, to get Rev into a better facility. As I was talking to Rev, I could hear the other patient in the room moaning so loudly as if in great pain. Please, JESUS, pour YOUR HEALING BALM upon this suffering soul.

**May 10, 2020, Sunday, 3rd day in Rehabilitation Facility:**
Prayer: *Dear JESUS, Thank You for the Blessing to rise to a New Day! I'm praying and fasting for Your Healing Balm upon Rev. LORD, please renew his strength. Please, LORD GOD, heal his whole-body frame.*

I called Rev. He seemed okay but somewhat confused. He sounded very sleepy.

Prayer: *Please dispatch Your Mighty Warrior Angels, Blessed SAVIOR, to be a shield of protection around Rev. Please guide this staff on how to care for Rev.*

"I am so thankful my sons are calling in to the virtual worship service at Smith Chapel on Sunday mornings! Please, LORD, create a hungering and thirsting to know You to have a personal relationship with You, JESUS.

Robinette and Dante came to visit me after service. They bought me a beautiful bouquet of tulips and a beautiful card for Mother's Day. I had completely forgotten it was Mother's Day. I don't know if I chose to forget because this is the first Mother's Day, I won't be able to spend it with Mother. I can't believe she's not here. Praying, she is rejoicing in the presence of CHRIST JESUS. Dante was busy taking care of things around the house: spraying Repel all around the front porch, letting both cars run for a while because they have been sitting for weeks. *Please bless Dante and Robinette, LORD, for their* loving *care of me.* Later, Dre came and brought gorgeous Mother's Day balloons and a beautiful card for me. He had a Mother's Day card for Mother. He went down to her room carrying the card and put it on her dresser. I let him go alone and spend time in her room. A searing pain pierced my heart and filled me with tears. (*LORD GOD, please comfort our grieving hearts.*) Dre also brought me a gift and a card from Lenora. They prepared a two-week supply of veggie bowls and snacks. So thankful for their thoughtfulness! Dre stayed for three to four hours. It was so comforting that he spent this time with me today. Please ALMIGHTY GOD bless Dre for all he does and for his kindness and love! Thank You HEAVENLY FATHER for blessing me with wonderful sons!

BLESSED SAVIOR I am reflecting back a few weeks ago on March 8, 2020 when Dre blacked out at home. He refused to go with the ambulance technician—said he felt okay. Rev persuaded him to go to the hospital. Doctors ran a series of tests that revealed his white blood cell count was level one when it should be a minimum of level four. Dre was hospitalized for a week. He was very weak and unable to work for two months. When Coronavirus tests were available, he was tested. Results were negative.

Prayer: *LORD GOD, my heart overflows with THANKS for YOUR HEALING BALM upon Dre! He's feeling so much better and able to return to work. Thank YOU, LORD JESUS, I am so grateful for Your HEALING MERCIES upon Dre.*

After several calls to Rev, I asked the receptionist to check if the phone was ringing in his room. I explained that he seemed a little confused when I talked with him earlier today. She asked for my number and said she would go to Rev's room and dial my number for him. I waited and waited. I never got the call. I called the switchboard, no answer.

Prayer: *"Merciful GOD, please heal Rev! Please protect Rev! Please guide the staff to provide the care he needs. YOU, O' GOD, are Rev's doctor! Please! Please! Heal Rev, BLESSED FATHER!"*

**May 11, 2020, Monday, 4th Day in Rehabilitation Facility:**

Prayer: *Blessed SAVIOR, Thank You, for the Blessings of this New Day! Please pour Your HEALING BALM upon Rev. Please strengthen Rev. I come to You, LORD, on bended knees, fasting and praying for Rev.*

I called Rev. As I was talking to him, he seemed very confused. I was glad the nurse came into the room. She said he had a good breakfast, and he was watching TV. I heard Rev talking to her, telling her he needed to take his clothes home and wash them, and he would bring them back tomorrow. I told the nurse he was not talking as normal and seemed very confused. The nurse said he won't keep oxygen in his nose. She said she's going to turn it up a little, and in about five minutes, he will be talking like himself.

Prayer: *LORD, please dispatch Your Warrior Angels to Protect Rev.*

I called Lori Parson, the case worker, at Charles Regional Hospital; she said that she was checking into a different facility and would call me later this afternoon. She called back around 1:30 p.m. Lori spoke to a social worker at the rehabilitation center to get current data on Rev available to forward to NRH or Good Samaritan Rehabilitation Center. She said that either would contact me.

Prayer: *May Your Holy will be done, LORD JESUS. You are George DeFord's doctor. Please let Your Healing Balm be upon him. Please, please*

*ALMIGHTY GOD surround George DeFord with Your Mighty Warrior Angels, protecting him from all hurt, harm, and danger.*

I called Rev around 9 a.m. He was talking coherently. He sounded good! Thank You, JESUS! The nurse came in, so he said he would call me back. Rev called at 12:53 p.m.; we had a good chat and hung up when the therapist came into the room.

Later that afternoon, I called Rev every few hours, but the phone just rang. After Intercessory Prayer time, I called Rev. I told him that the *Maryland Independent* wants to do an article about him as a Coronavirus survivor. I asked if he wanted to do it. He said it was okay, but I would have to do the talking. I asked if he had the oxygen (device) in his nose. He said he didn't know where it was. I called on my cellphone to speak to the nurse. I was told she was on her break and to call back in ten minutes. I stayed on the line with Rev because I wanted to make sure that the oxygen device was in his nose before I hung up. Rev kept talking about wanting to swim so he could strengthen his muscles. He wanted to know if the community college had reopened the pool. I called Lay Minister Perry, IT supervisor at the College of Southern Maryland to ask if the swimming pool had reopened. He said the college's in-person training was closed, and they were already making plans for all classes to be online next semester. Rev talked with Perry, commending him and the ministerial staff for doing an outstanding job keeping the ministries of the church going. Perry said it was because they had a good teacher. Rev told him he missed church family; Perry told Rev they missed him too and are thanking GOD for his recovery. Rev said he just wants to be home with his 'Girlfriend and Wife, who is one and the same.' I told Perry I thought we'd better end the conversation now because I didn't know where this conversation was going (smile). I'm staying on the line with Rev because I want to be sure he gets the oxygen back in his nose. One of the aides came to his door to ask if he wanted something to drink. I told him to ask her about his oxygen tube. She said she would get the nurse. The nurse came to the room and said the tube was on the floor, and she was putting the tube back in his nose for now, but would get him another one. I had prayer with Rev and said that I would call in the morning.

Prayer: *Please, JESUS, Heal Rev. Please protect him. Please instruct and guide the staff on how to care for him. YOU, O' GOD, are his doctor. LORD GOD, please strengthen his whole body-frame, every bone, muscle, nerve, and cell in his body. Please, LORD, touch him with Your DIVINE-HAND OF HEALING.*

**May 12, 2020, Tuesday, 5th Day in Rehabilitation Facility:**

Prayer: *Dear JESUS, Thank You for the gift of a new day. Please, BLESSED LORD, let Your HEALING BALM flow from the crown of Rev's head to the soles of his feet. Please strengthen his lungs.*

We continue to fast and pray for a full recovery for Rev. I started calling Rev at 6 a.m., but the phone just rang. At 7:28 a.m., I sent a text calling all Prayer Praise Warriors to their battle stations for prayer for Rev. Sister Gwen Kent texted a beautiful, encouraging devotional, "I Rise Today". I finally was able to speak to the nurse and explained I had not been able to speak to Rev, the phone just rang. She got me connected to Rev. He sounded okay. He wanted me to contact Denise Barnes, president of the Morgan State University Southern Maryland Alumni Chapter (MSUSMAC), to find out what the chapter's plans were for the 'Annual Scholarship Dinner-Dance' and advise them that it would be several months before he could be active again. He also asked for the District Administrator Mrs. Medley's phone number, but he did not have a pencil to write it down. So, I told him I would call her and give his number. Later, when I talked with Rev, he wanted me to call our primary care physician, Dr. Swaby, for a recommendation for a rehabilitation facility. Rev's complaining is escalating about how much he dislikes this rehabilitation center. Dante and Robinette called and talked to him for about twenty minutes. Rev is really not himself. He is extremely negative. All he talked about was getting out of the facility and how much he dislikes it.

Prayer: *LORD, please help me, help Rev. Please heal Rev. Please strengthen his body and mind. JESUS, You are my GUIDE, and COUNSELOR. Thank You for Your Mercy and Blessings that cover us.*

**May 13, 2020, Wednesday, 6ᵗʰ Day, in Rehabilitation Facility:**
Prayer: *HEAVENLY FATHER, Thank You for Your loving kindness to gift us with this new day. Praying and fasting for Rev's complete healing. Please, LORD, strengthen his whole-body frame. Please pour Your Healing Balm upon Rev, flowing from the crown of his head to the soles of his feet. Please, LORD, dispatch Your Mighty Warrior Angels to protect Rev.*

I called Rev, the phone just rang. The staff assigned him a different number. He wanted to know what I am doing for him to be transferred to a different facility. I told him I had spoken to Ms. Parsons and the social worker at the rehabilitation center, and they were supposed to get back in touch with me this afternoon. Rev wanted to know if Dr. Swaby had a facility that he would recommend? I told him that the doctor was having the staff call me with information. Rev said he ate 90 percent of his food. The physical therapist had him walking on the parallel bars and said he did excellent. Rev wants me to talk to his brother and get information about a veteran rehabilitation facility that he could go to.

Prayer: *Please, LORD JESUS, help me. Rev dislikes this facility so much. I don't want him to regress. Please, LORD, open up the facility that will provide the treatment he needs, that will strengthen his body. LORD GOD, calm us as we wait on You to reveal Your will.*

**May 14, 2020, Thursday, 7th Day in Rehabilitation Facility:**

Prayer: *Dear JESUS, Thank You for arising to see a new day! Thank You for enabling Dante and me to fast and pray for Rev. Please, LORD GOD, keep Rev safe under the covering of Your Protection. Please heal Rev, every bone, muscle, tissue, nerves—his whole-body frame. I thank You, LORD, for everyone who continues to pray for Rev's healing.*

I talked with Rev; he sounds okay today. He really dislikes this rehabilitation center. He said the food is terrible. I tried to encourage him to eat it anyway, so that his body will be strengthened. We continue to have problems talking on the rehabilitation center's phone, so Rev dug through his things and found his cellphone. One of the nurses let him use her charger. I asked Rev about his roommate. I had not heard him moaning. Rev said he passed. LORD GOD, may his soul be resting with You. I spoke with the case worker; I inquired how much physical therapy my husband was getting because Rev complains that all he does is watch TV. The social worker said that she would check and have the therapist call me. I urged her to process the necessary paperwork so Rev could be transferred to a different facility that would provide more physical therapy.

Prayer: *LORD GOD, You are Rev's doctor. Please guide the rehabilitation staff on what to do to help Rev. Please strengthen his body. Please pour Your Healing Mercy upon him to strengthen his whole body.*

**May 15, 2020, Friday, 8th Day in Rehabilitation Facility:**

Prayer: *Blessed SAVIOR, Thank You for last night's rest and the gift of a new day. Thank You. Dante and I, and PPW, are praying and fasting for Rev's complete healing—restored to health better than before the virus. Nothing is too hard for You, LORD. Please pour Your Healing Balm upon Rev. Please guide the staff on how to care for him. Please comfort Rev.*

I called Rev. He said he was okay. He's very embarrassed about his lack of bladder control. I told him it was probably because he had been catheterized for weeks in the hospital and that his body needs time to adjust. I told him to thank GOD his kidneys are working! I told him he knows how to pray and ask GOD to heal his body. He agreed.

Rev said his cellphone battery was at 30 percent. I told him I would contact his youngest brother, Terry, to ask him to buy a charger and carry it to him. I always end each conversation with a prayer for GOD's healing mercies upon Rev.

I spoke with Terry, and he said that he would carry a charger to Rev today. I asked him to go in his sheriff's uniform, and they might let him see Rev. I was not prepared for Rev's call this afternoon. Rev asked me to order him a pizza and chicken wings. I told him I didn't know which pizza company was near the rehabilitation center. He told me it's Domino's. I asked how was he going to pay for it. Rev said he had money. I told him I would check with the receptionist. I was relieved when I was told that they are not allowing any deliveries because of COVID-19. LORD, thank You for patience. Rev's focus seems to be on either getting out of this facility or on what foods he can get.

Prayer: *Please, LORD, heal Rev. Please strengthen his body, so he will be able to walk. Please pour Your Healing Balm upon him.*

**May 16, 2020, Saturday, 9th Day in Rehabilitation Facility:**

Prayer: *Dear JESUS, I am coming before Your throne of grace with a grateful heart. Thanking You for the gift of a new day; thanking You for the privilege to pray and fast for Rev's complete healing. Please, LORD, strengthen his whole body-frame, every bone, muscle, tissue. Please heal his lungs and breathing.*

I called Rev today. He said that he had a headache. I told him I would call the nurse. He said he was bored and sick of the limited TV channels available. I called and spoke to the nurse. She said they would give Rev a Tylenol.

Prayer: *LORD, please be a shield of protection around Rev. Please guide the staff as to how to care for him.*

**May 17, 2020, Sunday, 10th Day in Rehabilitation Facility:**
Prayer: *Dear LORD, Thank You for this Blessed Day. Please, JESUS, pour Your Healing Balm upon Rev. Please dispatch Your Mighty Warrior Angels to protect Rev. You, LORD, are Rev's doctor. Please instruct the staff on how to care for Rev.*

Rev called me at 5:30 a.m. He said he was feeling okay, but he didn't have anyone to call, so he called me. I asked if he had a headache this morning. He said, "No." Thank You, JESUS. I talked with him until they brought his breakfast. They persist in bringing him eggs even though I've told them he does not like eggs and does not eat eggs.

Prayer: *Please, LORD, heal Rev and please strengthen his whole body. JESUS, I know Your Hand of Healing is upon Rev and that You are working things out for his good. He's been so active, and it's extremely difficult for him to adjust to be confined in bed. Please give him patience to wait on You, for You are with him—with me! You are our strength, guide, and protector.*

**May 18, 2020, Monday, 11th Day in Rehabilitation Facility:**
Prayer: *Blessed SAVIOR, I thank You for the gift of a new day! Dante and I, and PPW are fasting and praying for Rev's healing. Please, LORD, strengthen his whole body-frame.*

Rev called me at 3 a.m., terribly upset because the aide had yelled at him. He said that he told her he was not a child. He was so upset; all I could understand was that it was an issue about bladder control and Depends. He said he wanted out of this place! I tried to calm him and assured him I would talk to the social worker and nurse.

Prayer: *LORD GOD, please help me! Please help Rev! Please protect Rev! I don't want him to regress! I was praying the physical therapy would help him to be able to walk again, but he's only had a few therapy sessions, and that has been at my insistence. I don't know how I'm going to be able to care for Rev by myself when he's unable to walk, but with Your help, LORD JESUS. By Your Loving Gracious Hand upon us, we will be able to do it!*

I called the social worker and told her Rev was terribly upset with the night staff because they were yelling at him. She said she would have the supervising nurse call me. The supervising nurse never called. When I talked with Dante, he said that he talked with Rev and thinks it's best for Rev to come home. (LORD, all is in Your Hands, please guide me and help me.)I called Rev at 5:30 p.m. and stayed on the phone until 11 p.m. to help calm Rev and to see how the night staff was going to treat him.

Prayer: *Please dispatch Your Mighty Warrior Angels to protect Rev. Please, Merciful LORD, pour Your Healing Balm upon Rev, touching every fiber of his being. You, O' GOD, are Rev's doctor! You have given us this miracle, restoring his life! Please, LORD, we look to You because You have never failed us!*

**May 19, 2020, Tuesday, 12th Day in Rehabilitation Facility:**
Prayer: *Dear JESUS, thank You for the gift of this new day. I know You, LORD GOD, have dispatched Your Warrior Angels to surround Rev and are protecting him from all hurt and harm. Please, LORD, continue*

*to let Your Healing Balm strengthen Rev. We are grateful, LORD, for Your unfailing love, grace and mercy. You, O' GOD, are our peace and comfort, our refuge in the storm.*

"I told Rev I had been calling the social worker, and left messages, informing her to make the necessary arrangements for his discharge on tomorrow. I made five calls to the case worker before she spoke with me. I asked about arrangements for oxygen. She said she would check with the nurse for me to hold while she spoke to the nurse. She said the nurse would schedule an oxygen test tonight and would have the results in the morning. If Rev required oxygen, it would have to be ordered by their doctor. I asked again if Rev could be tested for the virus, and she said they are not authorized to test when a patient is going home."

Prayer: *LORD GOD, thank You. I am grateful that You have stood with me to help me. I pray Your Hands of Healing will strengthen Rev's lungs and make his breathing easier.*

I'm gathering clean clothes to carry him. I don't know if they will give the clothes to Rev, so I am carrying his bathrobe. Dre said I should carry bedroom slippers, also. LORD JESUS, I am so excited! Tomorrow morning, we're going to Baltimore to get Rev and bring him home. I know I have to practice safe distancing, especially since we don't know if Rev is still positive or if I am. I will be sleeping on the living room sofa because the other bedroom, which was Mother's, room doesn't have the bed set up because she was using a hospital bed, which had been returned to the rental company.

Prayer: *THANK YOU, LORD GOD! This is yet another wonderful, amazing blessing You have bestowed upon us! Rev is coming home tomorrow! LORD JESUS, I am so Thankful! So Grateful! It's all because of Your Loving Kindness. I Praise and Glorify Your Holy Name!*

**May 20, 2020, Wednesday, 13ᵗʰ Day in Rehabilitation Facility:**

Prayer: *HEAVENLY FATHER, this blessed new day is here! Thank You for Your love that surrounds us—heals us—sustains us!*

Prayer: *I could not sleep last night! So excited! We are bringing Rev home today! I'm thinking about all that has happened, and I am amazed at Your Divine Hand overshadowing us! Our souls are rejoicing, brimming over with Praise and Adoration to You, ALMIGHTY GOD who loved us to life! Praise Your Holy Name!*

I've packed everything Rev might need: underclothes, socks, shoes, sweatpants, a facemask, and bags for his belongings and his dirty clothes.

Dante and I were on our way at 9:45 a.m. I requested to have Rev ready for discharge by 11 a.m. While we were on our way, the social worker called saying the results from the breathing test last night indicated Rev did not need oxygen. Praise You SAVIOR!! THANK YOU! Another Miracle from You, LORD JESUS!! We called the rehabilitation center to let them know we're parked at the front entrance. We were not allowed in, nor would they accept the clothes we had bought for Rev. He was brought out in a wheelchair, looking disheveled. No matter, I just hugged and kissed him. So happy to see him … to tell him I missed him and love him.

Prayer: *LORD JESUS, THANK YOU, LORD JESUS, THANK YOU!!! ALL PRAISES AND HONOR BELONGS TO YOU ALMIGHTY GOD, HALLELUJAH!!!*

Rev was so weak that he could barely stand. Dante and I had a tough time getting Rev into the car. I wrapped a robe around him. I put socks on him. But his feet were so swollen, I couldn't get his shoes on. I'm glad Dre suggested I bring his bedroom shoes. I put his mask and seat belt on, and we were ready to go home! Praise You, JESUS! Praise Your Holy Name!

Although Rev is physically weak, his mind is clear; he was giving driving directions for shorter routes home. Also, in spite of being physically weak, it hasn't affected his craving for food. He wanted a crab cake from the Blue Dolphin Restaurant (well known for its jumbo crab cakes). So, I placed an order for a carryout crab cake dinner for Rev.

Thank You, Merciful GOD, for traveling grace and mercy. We are home! Rev is so weak. Once Dante and I helped Rev up the three steps into the house, I had to get Mother's rolling walker so he could be rolled to the bathroom. The first thing he wanted was a shower. Afterward, a couple bites of the crab cake and he was ready for bed.

Prayer: *LORD JESUS, You have seen my tears, heard my fervent prayers, and You have loved us to life! You have heard all the prayers that have come to Your throne of grace from our family, church family, PPW, and friends. You, Blessed SAVIOR, revived us! Restored us! Our souls are overwhelmed with Joy—we are so Grateful—so Thankful—we are forever Praising, Worshiping and Glorifying You, our Blessed SAVIOR!*

**June 3, 2020, Wednesday, 14<sup>th</sup> Day at home:**

Prayer: *Dear JESUS, I greet You this morning with a heart overflowing with Praise and Thanks! We are so Grateful for Your Hand of Healing upon Rev. This is his 14<sup>th</sup> day home from the rehab center.*

We begin each day with prayer, reading the Scriptures and devotionals: *Our Daily Bread, Upper Room,* and a couple of other gifted devotionals. Normally, we would have our morning prayer time separately because Rev is an early riser. He would get a cup of coffee and go to his office to pray and prepare his sermons. Since Rev is still very weak, he's unable to go up and down the stairs. He needs the security of the walker to go from room to room. He's able to take care of his personal needs. Our daily routines have changed. I am administering all his medications and recording dates and times of the doses. I'm recording his vital statistics: blood pressure, temperature, and oximeter readings.

Dante continues to come daily to help me with various chores and take me to the military base to get Rev's medicine, groceries at the commissary, and to the credit union.

Prayer: *Please Bless Dante for his constant love and care. LORD, please open the windows of heaven and pour blessings upon Dante and Robinette for all they are doing to help us.*

Dre, Lenora, Dante, and Robinette prepared meals for us—a week's supply of cooked food. THANK YOU, LORD, for them! Please Bless them for their thoughtfulness and kindness to us.

Rev is struggling to remember what has happened in the past couple of months, and he's concerned about his hands trembling. I told him I think it's a side effect of the virus because my hands trembled also, but it eventually went away.

We received over a hundred cards, which I placed in a box unread until Rev came home, so we could read them together. Today, after dinner, I began reading cards to Rev. I started writing thank you cards. He put the TV on. I haven't had the television on since he's been sick. He began making grunting sounds. I thought it was because he didn't like the sci-fi movie he was watching. He asked me to get him a baby aspirin. As I was giving the aspirin to him, I asked what was wrong. He said that he did not feel good and his heart was racing. I took his pressure. It was 208/98. I called our doctor, who told me to call 911 right away. I called and was instructed to give Rev two more aspirins. I helped Rev sit in the living room near the front door. He began vomiting. The ambulance arrived quickly. EMS technicians took his pressure and asked if he could walk to the front door. The EMS technician assisted Rev to the front door, where they had the stretcher ready. I am beside myself. I am deeply agitated and upset. I'm shaking with anxiety and frustration. LORD GOD, HELP ME! Please, LORD GOD, HELP Rev! The ambulance did not pull off right away. I went outside and looked in the back windows and around to the front and all the way around the ambulance. I was trying to see what they were doing. Both the driver and the other technician were both working on Rev! I kept walking around the ambulance with my hands raised up to heaven. I was crying and praying, JESUS BLESSED SAVIOR, HAVE MERCY. Please help Rev! Please Help the technicians to help Rev. Please Guide them, LORD GOD, I'm calling on Your Holy Name, MASTER SAVIOR. Please Have Mercy on George DeFord. I kept circling around the ambulance, praying and crying so loudly that the next-door neighbor came to the door to ask what was wrong and if she could help. It seemed the ambulance had been in the driveway for ten to fifteen minutes. Another ambulance pulled up in front of the house, and then a third one. As the crew from the second ambulance walked up to the one in the driveway, she asked, "What's that terrible smell?"

The second crew member assisted the first ambulance EMS crew working on Rev, and they finally got ready to take him to the hospital. They told me the hospital would call me about Rev's status. The second and third ambulances stayed in front of the house because they identified the smell as gas. They called the fire department and called my propane provider. The technician spoke very encouragingly to me and suggested that I should go inside and close my garage door so the smell of gas would not go inside the house. He assured me they would stay until the gas leak was fixed and he would keep me updated. I continued praying, crying out to my REDEEMER SAVIOR to please have mercy on Rev!!.

Prayer: *LORD GOD ALMIGHTY, please be with Rev! Please Heal him, JESUS. You've brought him so far. Please, LORD GOD help us!*

I called Dante and Dre. Dante said that he would be right over (he lives ten to fifteen minutes away). I told him not to come—just pray. I told him he wouldn't be able to get into the neighborhood or park because there were five or six emergency vehicles lining the cul-de-sac.

Prayer: *Please, JESUS, guide doctors, nurses, and technicians of health as to what to do! Please, LORD, touch Rev with YOUR DIVINE HAND OF HEALING! LORD GOD, You, raised Rev up from a deathbed! Please, Please, LORD JESUS, help Rev!*

The ambulance technician rang the doorbell. He said the propane company man had not come yet, but he used to work for one of the propane companies. He checked my propane tank and saw that something was jammed, so he fixed it. The technician told me not to worry; there was no more leakage. THANK YOU, LORD JESUS. Please Bless this young man!

The propane company called and said their technician was on the way, and he arrived around 11:30 p.m. He checked the system, and there was no leak, and it was operating correctly. The hospital staff called; they stated that Rev was resting comfortably. His heart rate was better. As soon as the doctor reviews the test results, they would call me. At 1:45 a.m., hospital staff called and said Rev was ready for discharge, and he should follow up with a cardiologist.

Prayer: *JESUS! LORD GOD! HEAVENLY FATHER! How can I THANK YOU! How can I PRAISE YOU enough! You and You, alone, are Rev's DOCTOR! You are the Great Physician! You are his heart regulator! I PRAISE and WORSHIP YOU, for YOUR LOVE, YOUR GRACE and MERCY! You have heard and answered my prayers! I'm filled with THANKS and PRAISE. SO GRATEFUL! SO GRATEFUL!*

Dante picked up Rev from the hospital at 2:15 a.m. Rev was at home and feeling well!

Prayer: *All Praise to ALMIGHTY GOD!!*

# MY AFTERMATH REFLECTION, 2020

Reflecting on all that transpired in our lives from the beginning of 2020 until now, truly, our survival was miraculous. We were on our knees in prayer, welcoming in the New Year when the clock struck twelve! We prayed for blessings upon our loved ones and family; unity in a nation, divided; and for peace all over the world.

It had been only a few days later that the joyous beginning of the new year was shattered. On January 9, 2020, Mother fell and broke her hip, resulting in surgery on January 11th. She was in the hospital and subsequently in rehabilitation until the 28th. On February 16th, I blacked out and fell; I was hospitalized for one day, March 8th. Our oldest son, Andre (Dre), fell and blacked out and was hospitalized for a week identified with a low white blood cell count. On April 2nd, Mother was hospitalized and diagnosed with a stroke and COVID-19. I fell and blacked out, hitting my head on April 6th. Rev and I were diagnosed with the Coronavirus on April 8th, and Rev was admitted to the hospital. Mother passed on April 10th. Rev remained in the hospital until May 8th, when transferred to a rehabilitation center in Baltimore, MD and was discharged on May 20th.

This had been an extraordinary year of severe sickness, grief, and pain. In all my seventy-plus years, I do not recall such a time when we were confronted with such a succession of tragic family events! I've always prayed and lifted up all of my concerns, small and large, in prayer, but the year of 2020 brought me to my knees in unceasing prayer!

If anyone doubts the reality of GOD, I can testify unequivocally, GOD is REAL! I sought HIM in the most desperate times of my life, and GOD NEVER FAILED me. My soul is filled with PRAISE AND REVERENCE for ALMIGHTY GOD for HIS LOVING HAND OF HEALING GRACE and MERCY!

**In the midst and fresh aftermath of my pain, I offered the following prayer:**

*Heavenly FATHER, it is now seven months since Rev has been home recuperating. He has regained the fifty pounds that he lost during the time he was hospitalized and in rehab. He is well and walks almost every day, about a mile! It is Your constant touch of Healing upon Rev that has restored him! We are continuously Thanking and Praising You for this precious Miracle of Life!*

*Merciful GOD, I am persistent in Prayer, bombarding heaven with petitions for healing persons all over the world who are suffering from the Coronavirus and all other illnesses and diseases. The psalmist reminds us, "(You) heal all of (our) diseases." (Psalm 103:3b) I am convinced when we come to You in heartfelt prayer, You, will not only hear us, You, LORD GOD, will answer us in Amazing and Miraculous ways. Again, I point to Your Psalmist, "But truly God has listened; he has given heed to the words of my prayer. Blessed be to God, because he has not rejected my prayer or removed his steadfast love from me." (Psalm 66:19, 20) The Holy Scriptures are filled with Your promises to be with us at all times and in all situations.*

*As for the Prayer Praise Warriors (PPW) in the persons of Gwendolyn Kent and Stephanie West, that You, ALMIGHTY GOD, commissioned to fast and pray for Rev until he was completely healed. I thought we would return to our regular activities! Not so! The HOLY SPIRIT has assigned us to continue to intercede at Your Throne of Grace and Mercy as You direct us. The Scripture says, "... be unceasing and persistent in prayer." (1 Thessalonians 5:17 AMP) and "Make your life a prayer." (1 Thessalonians 5:17 TPT) Thanks be to God for this journey!*

CHAPTER 4

# REACTIONS FROM FAMILY, CHURCH, COLLEAGUES, AND FRIENDS

"Are any among you sick? They should call for the elders of
the church and have them pray over them, anointing them
with oil in the name of the Lord. The prayer of faith will
save the sick, and the Lord will raise them up"
(James 5:14, 15)

The news media typically captures the reactions of family members
who have lost loved ones due to the Coronavirus. Few record the
existential feelings of family and friends of those in the throes of
sickness and recovery. With this in mind, we present reactions and
reflections from those connected to us in various areas of our life experience.

The COVID-19 infection created quite an impact upon the social
milieu that Lila and I functioned within family, church, organizations,
and friends. The typical immediate reactions were anxiety and fear,
followed by interceding on behalf of the sick to God for healing mercy.

The Holy Scriptures attest to the benefit of praying for the sick, hence the scriptural reference in the heading of this chapter, in which the writer points to the elders of the church to come and pray for the sick. Nelson Cousins opined that patients healed especially when the attending physician laid hands upon the patient.[1] So it is when patients are cognizant of family and friends praying for them.

My wife and I collected a variety of reactions from family, church members from our current and previous appointments, clergy colleagues, classmates, alumni, and friends. We shared the comments and reflections (in real time and with soft edits), some in full and others in part. The reader can absorb the depths of anxiety, fear, and other emotions expressed by the individual writers.

## Family Reactions

**Andre, our oldest son, shared his reactions to our plight:**
The saddest and most spiritually uplifting moments in my entire life happened in April and May of this year (2020). The devastating loss of our 97-year-old beloved grandmother to COVID-19 was just the beginning. My Mother, Lila DeFord, and Dad, Rev. George DeFord, were also stricken with the virus. While "Ma" was sent home to self-quarantine alone, "Rev" was kept at the hospital due to shortness of breath. I remember so vividly how I felt about what my mother was feeling, having to go home sickened with the virus and overwhelmingly having to deal with the loss of her mother, who lived with her for [five] years, at the same time worrying about her husband, who was kept at the hospital! It almost seems unimaginable that this can happen. Ma had to walk past Grandma's bedroom to go to her room, and I know

the tears could not have stopped flowing! Ma, during this time, only allowed me one visit as she struggled with the virus. We, my girlfriend, Lenora, and I, came to her bedroom window as Ma pulled the blinds up and looked out. I will never forget, as long as I live, how my mother's face was stricken with grief, tears, and happiness.

We told her, "We love you," and "everything is going to be alright!"

She responded with, "I love you both," and waved. The moment only lasted a few seconds.

I left with tears of happiness and concern. Never witnessing before, my mother, looking so distraught. I simply could not imagine all the emotions and feelings she experienced being in the house all alone. My brother, Dante, was the angel our family needed to care for Ma during her time of healing. If it were not for Dante bringing Ma nourishment to sustain her and checking on her daily, I am not sure Ma would survive. But through God's grace and love, Ma beat the virus! However, Rev's condition was worsening, being put on a ventilator and then dialysis. Ma became a *Prayer Warrior*, summoning church members, family, and friends to send prayers up mightily on Rev's behalf. I remember never having prayed so intensely on my knees during Rev's battle with COVID-19. I felt like we were all connected together as one voice in communication with God.

When the doctors had expressed that there was nothing more they could do, Ma replied, "God will have the last say!"

All I can say is the power of prayer is undeniable. God delivered Rev from the clutches of COVID-19. Hallelujah!! God is great all the time! Ma and Rev are living happy and healthy today … God Bless!

—ANDRE

**Dante, our younger son and caregiver, wrote his perspectives:**

If I had to summarize the Coronavirus and the way it has affected my family over the past year, it would be, in a word, a *rollercoaster*.

It began around March 28th, when I called Ma to tell her that I was coming over to install new smoke detectors in their house, and she told me not to come because everyone over there had colds. I told her that I was coming anyway and proceeded to go and install the devices. I had no idea that everyone in the house had already contracted the Coronavirus, but it would also be the last time that I would see my grandmother before she passed.

I installed all the devices, never taking precautions not to contract their colds, in fact, I kissed my mother and grandmother upon seeing them. Before leaving, I kissed Grandma a second time when she asked me what I thought would come of this pandemic. I told her, "Grandma, this will pass in a while, and we'll be back doing the same thing we used to do." She laughed a little. I left and never saw her again. A day or so later, Ma informed me that Grandma had to go to the hospital because she was hallucinating. It all got crazy after that.

On or about April 6, at approximately 6 a.m., Rev unsuccessfully attempted to phone me, but I did not hear the call (because I typically silence my cellphone at night). I believe I may have gotten up to use the bathroom and looked at my phone (which I often do) and saw a missed call from him; that's when it all started. I was informed by Rev that Ma had passed out and hit her head pretty badly and was bleeding profusely. Rev's temperament was panicked but at the same time kind of *out of it*. I began to get panicky and asked if he had called the ambulance, to which he replied, "Yes, they [are] on the way."

I got up to get dressed and called again. Rev then informed me that the ambulance was taking Ma to the hospital. Later that day, Robin and I picked Ma up from the hospital after having staples placed in her head; her nightgown was covered in blood, and she looked really disconnected, like she was in a daze. We took Ma home.

Testing was imminent. To Robin's insistence, both Ma and Rev got tested for COVID-19, a day or so later, both came up positive, which resulted in Rev being hospitalized for at least a month, and Ma being on her own to recover at home. Without completely chronicling everything at this point, it came down to making sure that Ma was preparing for the worst; she was scared but always brave enough to walk it on her own. Ma never asked for anything, but we as a family wanted to make sure that she had whatever she needed, i.e., prayers, fasting, food, vitamin supplements, etc.

Rev's health was declining rapidly, but before being put into a coma-like state, he had a conversation with me about his final wishes. I listened, but I wasn't ready to hear that. I always felt GOD would deliver them both from this disease. (Oddly enough, Grandma and Rev's rooms were right next door to each other, and they didn't even know it.) I couldn't believe that after so many blessed years in this family that it could all end like this. Needless to say, between Rev's daily condition reports from the hospital (mostly unfavorable) and Ma's home recovery, it was a very tense time.

We received the news that Grandma transitioned, which was devastating. She truly was the matriarch of this family. We will never stop missing her, but believing in GOD's promises, we know she is in a better place!

Ma, over the next month, slowly but surely got stronger (a real soldier), she refused to be what she considered to be a burden to us. (She never could be.) I remember Ma tirelessly dealing with the hospital to ensure Rev's recovery; there were a lot of very emotional days.

GOD heard and answered our prayers because, in true miracle fashion, GOD delivered them both back to us, and their recovery was nothing less than astonishing.

My main takeaway from this is that first, you can't pray and worry; do one or the other. Secondly, GOD doesn't want you to live in fear, so give it to him and do what you have to do. I am just beginning to sleep at night without worrying about my phone going off with an emergency. Those calls scared me, but I had to rely on faith through it all. My last statement is that my family believes that I'm hardcore in the way I come off, but I do truly love and care about all of us; I just do it in my own way.

Thank you, GOD, that my parents were given their lives back, I want them to enjoy many more happy and healthy years together.
—DANTE

\* \* \*

And here's where I'd like to share how our son's account of his grandmother's ordeal and eventual passing, and mine and Lila's COVID battle, could serve as an example of secondhand trauma. Dante combined several incidents involving Mother, Margaret McRae, and my wife, Lila. In December 2019, Mother fell while trying to get out of bed and fractured her hip, which required hospitalization. In January 2020, while Mother was in Sagepoint Rehabilitation in La Plata, MD, on a Sunday morning as Lila and I were getting ready for church, Lila blacked out and hit her head against our bedroom's armoire, causing a large gash. An Ambulance had to rush her to the hospital. On April 6, 2020—two days before Lila and I had to go to the hospital due to illness—Mother was diagnosed with COVID-19 and admitted to the hospital, eventually transitioning on April 10, 2020, at 5 p.m.

\* \* \*

**Robinette, Dante's wife and our daughter-in-law, averred the following:**

I can't say that this was not a scary moment in time because it was!! I watched Dante be his strongest as he struggled with the loss of Grandma and pushed through his feelings to care for his mom and Rev—to the best of his abilities. I felt Ma mustering all her strength while physically feeling her worst, knowing that her mom had transitioned without any family member there, and knowing that Rev wasn't at his best in the hospital. She still limited access to herself by quarantine and isolation. That's being strong. Then, Rev, I can only imagine how he pulled through with his strength. But he did!!! This unbelievable moment put us on our knees, day and night. Thank You, Merciful God, for hearing and answering our prayers with favor.

Amen!

—ROBINNETTE

**Dianna, my youngest sister, wrote:**

When I learned that my eldest brother George had been diagnosed with COVID-19, I was filled with fear. Having observed my husband go through the virus, I became acquainted with some of the signs of the virus and its effects on the human body.

When I learned that you had been hospitalized and later, we could not speak with you or get information about you from the hospital, I became even more afraid. Lila gave us daily updates, but we (siblings) could only pray for you. As the days progressed, the news became even more ominous. For certain, I knew that I was going to lose my big brother. You were always my hero, champion, and rescuer. You had stepped up in our family to assume the role of the patriarch when Daddy died. Two years ago, you gave me away at my wedding. You had attended my college graduations and visited me in the hospital at the births of my daughters. Earlier in our lives, you were the big brother who was always around. You made family gatherings special—simply by your presence. As your life in the ministry grew, we (family) were so proud of you and all your accomplishments. I can remember Daddy saying, "Don't you want to go to college like your Big Brother?"

I could not fathom life and our family without you. You have always been a special breed of a person. As a family, we got to share so many special moments with you. I was not ready for that to end.

I was grateful for Lila's updates, her prayers for you, her fasting, and her unwavering faith that God would heal you. Despite how ominous the reports from the hospital were, Lila remained steadfast in her prayers for your healing. I have developed an even greater love and respect for her as your wife. She never gave up hope. Please know this: you and Lila are well-loved and respected by our family. We treasure both of you as God's gift to our family. We, Billy, Travia, Terry, Dennis, Darlene, Larry, and I, are eternally grateful to God for healing you and giving us more time on the planet with you.

Much Love to you, Big Bro.

—Baby-sis, Di

**Dennis, the fraternal twin of Dianna, and Darlene, my sister-in-law, wrote:**

While watching and listening to all the news reports, our hearts would go out to all those individuals suffering from COVID-19. Then, noticing how it was affecting our seniors, in particular, I never imagined that it would affect our family. My oldest brother contracted the Coronavirus. How could this happen, the brother whom I looked up to and admired? The one Darlene would tease and say, "I bet you,

Franklin, has a pop-up or idea about something." The reality was we were afraid, afraid of the unknown and not knowing. As anxiety began to set in, not being able to talk with your loved ones or visit them, and not having control over anything, made for moments of fear along with restless nights.

Then we had to realize that no matter what, we could go to our Heavenly Father. We had to stretch out our faith and know that God is able to do all things. So, as we prayed and solicited the prayers of others, we knew that everything would be okay. Our constant prayer was asking God to do what only He can do, that is, to heal and restore our Big Brother's health.

—DENNIS AND DARLENE

**Terry DeFord, the youngest sibling, wrote:**

I was very worried when I found out that my brother, George, was in the hospital being treated for the Coronavirus. It had finally hit home; most of the stories that I heard were on the news about people I did not know, and the current political administration, dampening the severity of the virus, saying it was not that bad, so I was very worried, not knowing what the outcome was going to be with my brother's health. My siblings and I look up to George; he is the eldest of our immediate family. George and I were born on the same day (October 7th), but 22 years apart. I thought that was so incredibly unique in our family that he and I shared the same birthday.

Matters seemed to be getting worse. George's wife, Lila, advised the family that he has been transferred to the ICU unit and has been placed on a ventilator, and soon after that, he was on dialysis. She asked the family to pray fervently that the Lord will restore his health. I shared the grim news with my cousins on both sides of the family and with the members of Enon Baptist Church, where George received his early Christian training as a youth. I began to reach out to other Christian friends to ask them to pray for my brother. My family felt so helpless, we could not come to visit him because of the health regulation with the COVID-19, but that we serve an omnipresent God who will be with our beloved brother every step of the way.

I communicated with my sister-in-law to get updates on my George's prognosis, [but] little seemed to change. She would always say, "Continue to pray for George that the Lord will bring him through," and she firmly held on.

I was encouraged by her faith, knowing that her beloved Mom, Mrs. McRrae, had recently passed. Lila remained faithful to George's health, being restored by the Lord. I thank God for giving her the strength to remain faithful in Him even after the passing of her mom, whom we all loved.

Over two weeks had gone by, and George's prognosis remained the same. Relatives, church members, and friends would ask me, "How's your brother George doing?"

And I would say, "He's about the same; continue to pray for his health."

I found an old photo album in my house with pictures of George. I began to wonder if I would ever see him again.

One day, I returned home from work, and as I pulled into my driveway, my cell phone began to ring. I saw my sister Dianna's name on the caller ID. I braced myself and answered the phone: "Hello."

"Hey Terry!"

I said to myself, *she sounds exuberant.* I somberly replied, "Hey Diane."

She said, "Did you hear from Lila?"

I replied that my phone buzzed a couple of times while I was driving, adding, "I see that she was trying to call me. What's up?"

"Frank's making some progress!"

Growing up, George was called by his middle name, Franklin/Frank. "Really!" I was overwhelmed with joy. As the week went by, Lila was updating the family with more good news about our brother's continued progress and thanking and praising God for what He has done. I couldn't wait to share the good news with church members, relatives, and friends.

About a week later, I received a group email with a video attached showing my brother George being discharged from the hospital and all the healthcare workers cheering him on as a gurney was being strolled out to an awaiting ambulance. My church family was able to recover the video and share it on Zoom during our noonday prayer service. Everyone was excited and praised the Lord for restoring George's health from the Coronavirus. I continue to pray and thank God for restoring my brother George's health and giving him a strong and faithful wife.

—TERRY

**Sheila, Lila's sister, wrote:**

Lord, I'm thankful. I had one sister in the hospital with COVID-19, one sister at home alone with the same virus, and her husband in the hospital on a ventilator with COVID-19. I was scared of losing my sisters and brother-in-law. I prayed and reached out to my prayer warriors for healing for my family. God heard our prayers and brought them home. God is Good All the Time and All the Time, God is Good!

We were blessed, although COVID-19 touched my family, God's Grace and Mercy brought us through.

We pray for those families that have been touched by this virus and those that have lost loved ones and ask the Almighty God for strength through this difficult time in our nation.

—Sheila

**Shirley, Lila's sister and twin of Sheila, wrote:**

As the news around the world talked about this COVID-19 pandemic, it became a very scary thing for me. I was fearful and prayed that this virus would not affect my family. Yet, it affected my sisters and brother-in-law. I began praying every day for their healing to overcome this virus.

I'm scared, we just lost our mother, and my sister is home alone with the virus.

Lord God, I pray to please have mercy. My brother-in-law is in the hospital on a ventilator, fighting for his life.

I'm so thankful that GOD found favor in them and they have recovered from this deadly virus. I give God all the glory for watching over each and every one of us.

—Shirley

**Shauntia S., Shirley's daughter and our niece, rendered a touching reflection:**

Lord, have mercy!! Those were the only words of prayer that I could seem to utter when I learned that not only was my grandmother hospitalized with COVID, but two of my aunts, as well as my uncle, who eventually ended up on a ventilator.

I come from a praying family, but in that very moment, I felt myself struggling with exactly what to pray for, feeling weighed down with the heaviness of the unknown. The unknown of their conditions, the unknown if they would survive; totally at the mercy of nurses to provide updates. The feeling of hopelessness and helplessness was indescribable.

This very virus that we as a family talked about and watched through news media, how it was wreaking havoc on our nation, has now hit our very own doorstep. Sadly, we lost my grandmother, who succumbed to the virus, and my aunts and uncle are still healing from the effects of the Coronavirus.

As I reflect back, I realize that everyone, everywhere, was impacted. Regardless of race, ethnicity, socio-economic background, etc., we were all hit with COVID in some way or another. In the forced rest required by social distancing, I came to value even more the loving family I was birthed into. I have a greater appreciation for the simple moments of a conversation, a smile, and I miss the warm hugs of family members.

Life is indeed precious, and I'm thankful to God daily for the family members who survived and forever embrace the memory of our precious loved one who has gone on.

—SHAUNTIA

## CHURCH MEMBERS' REACTIONS

**Mrs. Nancy B. wrote:**

When I heard that both of you had COVID-19, I felt like my mother and father were sick and that there was not anything that I could do to help but just pray, and because I felt like I was that close to you and Mrs. DeFord. I thought about Rev. DeFord being in the hospital alone without Mrs. DeFord, your partner, your buddy, and your helpmate, which made me feel so sad.

I was so glad when Dante started giving us daily updates, and then Mrs. DeFord—when she was better.

Seeing that video of them wheeling you out of the hospital and seeing Mrs. DeFord not wanting to let you go, I cried and cried, then I thought, *when he gets well enough, I'm going to make him a lemon meringue pie.*

Love you both,

—Miss Nancy

**Audrey and Roland C., and Keisha C. wrote:**

When we heard the news that the DeFords and Mother had COVID-19, we were in shock, and after we found out that Reverend and Mother were hospitalized, and Lila was going home, we felt bad for her, thinking about her being alone.

Then we found out that Mother passed, and Reverend was on the ventilator; our hearts were broken; we loved Mother very much; she became like family to us also. We also felt bad about the fact that Lila and Reverend could not attend Mother Margaret's Celebration of Life Service (she lived with them, and they were her caregivers). I know that was hard for them.

We prayed a lot for them, especially Reverend.

When we could not contact Lila, I texted her every day and sent her scriptures and inspirational readings to help lift her spirit, but her focus was on fasting and praying for Reverend.

I will never forget the Sunday that I preached while Reverend was still hospitalized. At the end of the service, I prayed a special prayer for Reverend. I prayed like never before. Tears started rolling down my face, my husband and daughter looked at me, and I kept praying; my voice changed, and I kept praying. We prayed for him and Lila during our worship services every Sunday.

On Friday, May 8, 2020, after spending 30 days in the hospital, we received a video of Reverend being rolled out of the hospital. They stopped and let Lila kiss him while Dante and Robinette hugged him. We cried tears of joy for all of them. Every one of our church families that I spoke with felt the same way. Our prayers were answered. We knew (our pastor) was not going home, but he was out of the woods.

I know when the Reverend was able, he cried out to God, and He heard his prayers. 'A righteous man falls seven times and rises again' (Proverbs 24:16).

We, as a church, had the opportunity to drive by the DeFords' home on June 28, 2020, first time we had seen them since April 5th on Zoom. We spoke to them from a distance, and each one of us, and our youth, presented him with a token, pictures, and other items. During the drive-by, I had the opportunity to show (Pastor) my certificate, I received from the Certified Lay Ministers' class, that he encouraged me to take. I am glad I did.

We love and have the utmost respect for Reverend and Lila DeFord, and their family will forever be our family.

—ROLAND AND AUDREY C., AND KEISHA C.

**Mildred W. wrote:**

When I heard the news of the Pastor and First Lady being infected with COVID-19, I was devastated, not to mention extremely concerned and a little fearful for their well-being. Dante was keeping the church family up to date with their progress. When Mrs. DeFord came home, and the Pastor stayed, I was really upset.

Eventually, I was able to speak with Mrs. DeFord, and she mentioned that she was fasting and praying until noon for the Pastor. I volunteered to join her and asked permission to share with the congregation for those who could also join in as some cannot fast for health reasons. My thinking was that since they are our Pastor and First Lady, we should care enough to turn down the plate to ask God to restore health and healing to both of them. Mrs. DeFord shared healing scriptures, and I was able to download some as well. I read and prayed those scriptures pretty much daily and documented my concerns to God.

Blessings,

—Mildred W.

**Pete W., Staff Parish Relations Committee, Chair, wrote:**

I remember the fear I had when I heard the news that the Pastor and Mrs. DeFord had been infected. I kept thinking that there must be something my wife and I could do to help make them feel better. I knew how the Pastor felt about Smith Chapel, and I did not want him to be concerned; I wanted to somehow set his mind at ease so he could concentrate on fighting the virus.

I was conflicted about my feelings and concern for the Pastor and Mrs. DeFord because they are like family, and I wanted to know all the details that I had no right to know. I felt restricted, anxious, worried, and angry at times. Later, I began to think about what the Pastor taught from the pulpit and in Sunday School, and his faith in the Word. That gave me hope, which changed everything.

I cannot even explain the joy I felt when Mrs. DeFord came home and when I connected with Dante, the son, who kept me informed. Somehow, after that, I knew everything was going to be okay. I could see the love of God. Thank God for the DeFords being who they are.

—Pete

**Rachel S. J., a healthcare professional and lay minister, wrote:**

Early March 2020, I can remember when the alarm bells of the coming pandemic seemed to be far in the distance. Certainly not enough to cause panic for me. I am a health professional, a Certified Registered Nurse Anesthetist, and we will follow what the CDC guidelines are telling us. No need for masks, cover your cough, and practice adequate hand hygiene. It will be fine. This was the recommendation at the time, and I believed it.

For a few weeks, the schools would be closed, and people would stay home from work, church, and non-essential business, and then we could resume normal life. It will be fine. I was still planning an 18th Birthday/Graduation Party for my daughter, Olivia, for April 2020. My hope was that by then, it would truly be fine.

Then the numbers started to rise. New cases. Increased hospitalizations. More deaths. The alarms were louder, and I certainly had empathy and concern for the situation and those affected, but it was like watching a war being fought on a foreign land. The danger didn't seem that close as long as we had the guidelines.

And then the war was at my front door.

I remember receiving a group text from the church administrator, Ms. Vera L., saying that *Pastor and Mrs. DeFord were being seen at the hospital, both with COVID-19 symptoms.*

Subsequently, we received notice that both were diagnosed as COVID-positive. Knowing that the two beloved spiritual leaders of the church were suffering the effects of this disease made the danger of the pandemic clear and very present. While Pastor DeFord was being treated in the ICU, the church members collectively and separately fasted and prayed. We waited, admittedly sometimes anxiously, for progress reports. We shared in the concerns and rejoiced in the triumphs. The elation of knowing that he was off the ventilator, leaving the hospital, and returning home was indescribable.

For me, during this time, the strength and comfort I found in my faith community were extremely important. Though we could not meet physically, we continued to meet spiritually, worshiping, studying, and praying together by way of video conferencing. We also texted and called each other almost daily to check on one another and offer encouragement. We shared in each other's concerns during a time that was like no other.

Going through the experience of having our pastor become incapacitated so suddenly, in my opinion, has strengthened the bonds that we share as a congregation. During those tenuous days, we depended on each other. We were our brother's and sister's keeper.

—Rachel

**Vera L., church administrator, gave her titled reflection:**

## *The Void*

When Rev. and Mrs. DeFord were diagnosed with the Coronavirus, and he was in ICU and she had to be quarantined, basically, a hole was in my heart, and my spirit was on the verge of being helpless. Mrs. DeFord asked us to fast and pray for the healing; we had no idea our pastor was that ill.

Dante kept in constant contact with us as well. In this time, 'Mother' (Mrs. DeFord's mom) went home to be with the Lord. Truly, this was a very difficult time for me; she was my angel. When I did visit her at Sagepoint, we had a great conversation and shared, again, through prayer, that we made it.

The Pastor and First Lady were not just those titles assigned to Smith Chapel; they had become a very integral part of my family. We had a bond of friendship, and they had been a stabilizing factor in my spiritual growth, especially with the illness and passing of my mom, and then within 14 months, all her siblings. He was there for all of them to offer comfort.

Though we had several Certified Lay Ministers and Certified Lay Speakers to stand in as the District Superintendent, also to deliver the messages and to give guidance, the same level of love and support was not there, the VOID was, still and will be there. But by the GRACE of GOD, they are still here and still doing His works.

—VERA L.

**Dorothy M. and Gail M., Mother and Daughter, wrote:**

I did not think the DeFords would get so sick, but I also knew God was going to heal them. Everyone has so much love for them, and God answers prayers.

I felt very stressed by their diagnosis. I also felt helpless, because I couldn't help both Rev. and Mrs. DeFord. But the Lord heard my prayers by protecting and healing both of you.

—MAMA AND GAIL

**Veronica M., a/k/a *Elnora*, Church Council, Chair, wrote:**

When I heard the Pastor and Mrs. DeFord had come down with the Coronavirus, I was sad and concerned at the same time. I had so many questions but could not get the answers I wanted to hear. Once I heard Mrs. DeFord was recovering at home and getting better, some of the weight was lifted off my heart.

Prayers and texts from the church family came daily, and we prayed until God healed both of them.

—Ms. ELNORA

**Barbara W. wrote:**

I was devastated when the news came regarding Reverend and Mrs. DeFord, diagnosed with the COVID-19. I prayed that God would heal both of them and everyone else. Thank God my prayers were answered.

—BARBARA

**Alan R., active member of Sunday Church School, commented:**

When I first heard that Rev. DeFord had the Coronavirus, my mind began racing 100 mph. In the span of 30 seconds, I went through a wide range of emotions. Because we knew so little about the virus, fear immediately hit me. Would he survive? Would Mrs. DeFord catch it? Quickly, anger took over. I was mad because someone had the audacity to expose my friends, the DeFords, to the virus. I began to question *Why?* With no answer to *Why*, a sense of helplessness came over me. Could not visit, could not call. All I could do was pray. I think prayer helped me as much as it did the DeFords. A sense of resigned calm led to the feeling of hope that all would be OK.

—ALAN R.

**Jocelyn R., wife of Alan R., Certified Lay Minister and Worship Team Leader, wrote:**

The sadness started with me when I read the text to pray for the First Lady's mother, that she was not doing well. Then the text came that she had passed; it brought me to my knees. I so loved her; I could see her smile. I felt her loving Spirit as she would always encourage

110

me as she sat on the second pew at church. But the bad and sad text did not stop as the church's lay leader kept everyone updated. I was not prepared for the text when I read that the same time, how both Pastor and First Lady DeFord tested positive for COVID-19. I was at a loss for words. I did not understand what it meant to be tested positive, but this was Pastor. *This was only a test; it would pass.* Little did I understand the severity, [what it truly meant] to test positive for this thing called COVID-19. The test now would move to be the thing that almost caused Pastor his life. First Lady came home after testing positive; surely, Pastor would follow. Well, he was not sent home for a while. The unknown was scary to me. The church's little prayer turned to big prayer, because now the question was not when but if, now that Pastor was fighting daily for his life. I only knew more because of the church texts. The unwelcome news never let up. Because of the Pastor's condition, each text became more serious than the previous one. I remember one text from First Lady, out of many, asking us to just Pray, Fast, and Pray, because Pastor was now on oxygen, that even, she could not be with him. She later updated us that now Pastor was on dialysis, because his kidneys shut down. All the while having to sign papers for Pastor's life, in the event he would turn for the worse. But as a church family, we all came together, interceding, believing that God would bring our Pastor home. And He did, and He kept our First Lady still and in Prayer; that is who she is. I love you, Both, and thank God for His faithfulness. Bless God.

—JOCELYN R.

**Cheryl K., a member of Ebenezer UMC, Washington, DC, wrote:**
    When my mother told me that Rev. DeFord had the virus, I was frightened. People were dying from this virus. Rev. DeFord was our

111

former pastor. Former pastors … are forever family. They are part of the very fabric of the church's foundation …We met George DeFord when he was a young man and came to Ebenezer as an intern and was mentored by our beloved Rev. Dr. Alfonso J. Harrod. Some years later, Rev. DeFord returned to us to serve as our senior pastor.

We were overjoyed. While this appointment lasted a few years, Rev. DeFord's commitment and love toward the Ebenezer family extends decades. In August 2019, he performed the wedding ceremony for my daughter. So, Rev. Dr. George DeFord is family.

I started calling the family to solicit prayers. I called Mrs. Lester, Mary, Pat, Jimmy, and Marsha. I called Rev. DeFord's intern during the '90s, Rev. Dr. Deese, in South Carolina, and our son and former pastor, Rev. Dr. B. Kevin S., in Michigan. People were calling the house, and calling the house, and not getting any answer. Then we heard that our former first lady, Lila, had the virus as well. Calls were repeated, a formalized prayer chain was developed, and a search for additional information began. The hospital does not recognize the relationship between pastor and parishioner as familial. Weeks and weeks passed while Lila was home. Then one day, many of us were just watching the news and heard that a man was being released after weeks and weeks of being ill with the virus. We saw this man on a stretcher being rolled out, and all of a sudden, Lila ran to him. It was Rev. DeFord; he was okay. Well, I am normally a restrained Methodist. But Honey, I started shouting in here, crying, and thanking God that our Pastor wasn't in the number of thousands and thousands of poor souls who had lost their lives to this virus. We thank God for healing.

—CHERYL K.

# CLERGY COLLEAGUES

Rev. Dr. Johnsie W. Cogman, District Superintendent of the Washington East District, Baltimore-Washington Conference, of the United Methodist Church, gave a reflection titled, *The ABCs Effect of COVID*:

## Actualization of the affliction:

When I received the initial news of Rev. and Mrs. DeFord, contracting the Coronavirus, the news was devastating, to say the least. These were the first people that I knew personally who were diagnosed with COVID-19. The actualization of this deadly disease became much more real, but I had faith that both would survive. As the District Superintendent, I began to provide pastoral care to Rev. DeFord and his wife during this trying time. When the disease progressed within Dr. DeFord's body, he came to the realization that retirement from pastoral ministry was imminent. Thus, I had to assume the role as Interim Pastor of Smith Chapel United Methodist Church (UMC). Because of Dr. DeFord's exceptional leadership in developing dynamic leaders, it was a smooth transition to becoming Interim Pastor. The leaders stepped up, and mission and ministry continued as Smith Chapel continued to bless others.

## Blessings abound:

Despite the horror of COVID-19, blessings did abide during this time. There was the blessing of folks coming together to pray every day. There was an intentional effort to ensure that Dr. DeFord was covered in prayer every hour of every day while he was in intensive care. There was the blessing of the church leaders stepping up and ensuring the church continued as usual and never missed a beat. Interactive

Bible studies, transformative sermons, and wonderful worship were a reflection of the leadership that Dr. DeFord had developed. There was the blessing of cards and calls showing 100 percent support of First Lady Lila DeFord, while she suffered at home alone with not only the COVID-19 virus herself, but the loss of her mother to this deadly disease. I mailed her a handmade cross with the WED and JESUS on it, so that she would know she was loved by Jesus and the Washington East District. Sometimes, when we are in the midst of a crisis, we don't see any blessings, but when we look back over our lives, we can see God's blessings still abound over and over again.

### Confirmation that God is still in control:

After many days of prayer, there came a video that we shall always remember with joy in our hearts … Dr. DeFord, leaving the hospital having survived COVID-19! The video went viral throughout our district and the BWC [Baltimore Washington Conference]. Everyone rejoiced and gave God praise! It was confirmation that God hears and answers prayers! After a short stay in a rehabilitation center, Dr. DeFord went home and was able to have short conversations on the telephone as he gathered his strength back. After much prayer and discernment, a new pastor was appointed to take the reins for Smith Chapel and continue leadership. Dr. DeFord was able to meet in person with masks on and social distancing, with the new pastor, and pass the baton to his successor with joy and thanksgiving. This truly was confirmation that God is still in control.

Although many still struggle with this deadly disease, and many have lost their lives and the lives of their loved ones … I speak with a grateful heart, of the life of Rev. Dr. George DeFord, and the impact he has had not only on Smith Chapel UMC but the Washington East District.
—REV. DR. JOHNSIE W. COGMAN

## Rev. Dr. Eugene W. Matthews, pastor of St. Mark's UMC, Laurel, MD, wrote:

Thomas Paine, the author of the 1776 pamphlet, *Common Sense*, wrote words reflective of the crisis of the American Revolutionary War: 'these are times that try men's souls.' This predicament can aptly describe the current situation that exists in the world, our nation, and our communities relative to the scourge known as the COVID-19 Pandemic.

The reported cases of this virus began to rise by mid-March 2020; however, at that time, I was unaware of anyone who had contracted this disease. Soon after, either in late March or early April 2020, news circulated that the Deford family had become victims of this pandemic. Also, to my dismay, word was that Dr. George Deford had been hospitalized. Therefore, on Friday, April 10, 2020 (Good Friday), I telephoned the Defords' residence. Having been unable to reach anyone, I then proceeded to dial Dr. George Deford's cell number. Surprisingly, George answered, and with a haltering voice, he informed me that he was at that time receiving medical assistance and would call me later. I urged him not to return my call, but later that same evening, I contacted him on his phone, and the two of us briefly engaged in a conversation about his condition, which concluded with prayer. Subsequently, each Friday, a special prayer was lifted by me for Rev. Deford and his family since hearing that his mother-in-law had died. I reached out to other colleagues and asked them to do the same. This persistence continued until a few weeks later, on a Friday, I again reached out via telephone to the Defords' residence. This time, to my delight, Mrs. Lila Deford, wife (A.K.A. Girlfriend), answered and, in an emotional conversation, informed me that George was now on a respirator. My spirits sank and my anxiety increased because this is a colleague whom I have known and served with in ministry who was now in intensive care. Moreover, we had both served together as members and later as Chair of the Board of Ordained Ministry (BOOM) of the Baltimore-Washington Conference. Added to this was the fact that the DeFord family was highly active members of the Sharp Street Memorial U.M.C., Baltimore, Maryland, during my pastorate there. This was an additional link to our relationship.

But we fast forward to another experience as noted by the Psalmist: 'Weeping may endure for a night, but joy comes in the morning.' (Psalm 30:5) That joy came when on the evening of Friday, May 8, 2020, I phoned the DeFords' home to inquire about Dr. DeFord's health status, and to my delight, his 'Girlfriend' Lila answered the phone. And in a joyful voice, informed me that George had been released from the hospital that very day to a rehab center. What joy filled my heart, and I said to Mrs. Lila DeFord, "You will probably sleep well tonight." Their son, Dante, also sent a text to me later showing the release of George and Lila embracing him with the hospital staff, surrounding and applauding him as he left. Dante added in his text message that the staff said, 'This was a miracle.'

The Bible contains these recorded words, 'The prayers of a righteous man are powerful and effective ...' (James 5:16 NIV).

Thanks Be to God,

—EUGENE W. MATTHEWS

**Rev. Kermit C. C. Moore, Pastor, Providence-Fort Washington UMC, Fort Washington, MD, shared his thoughts:**

As a result of hearing daily news reports of the high number of deaths as a result of this disease, my first reaction to the hearing that Rev. DeFord and Ms. Lila both had contracted the Coronavirus was to say: "Oh No!" But then, later, after I thought more about this situation,

I began to remember the mighty power of the God we serve. I started to realize that there is nothing too hard for our God. Regardless of the age or pre-existing conditions, the God we serve is bigger than all those situations. I then started to rely on my faith more than the news reports. I started to rely on my hope more than the doctor's reports. It is times like these when one's hope and faith are tested. And of course, prayer always works as well!! In the end, Our God showed us once again who is the biggest Healer in the world!
—KERMIT MOORE

**Sandra E. Smith, Retired Local Pastor, wrote:**
COVID-19 has plagued America and other parts of the world for at least the past nine months. Millions of people have died, and multitudes hospitalized or quarantined at home. The pandemic has produced a climate of anxiety, depression, and an increasing distrust in America's current administration.

Despite this environment, there are persons who have survived COVID-19, after being hospitalized and in a coma for sometimes more than several weeks. Rev. George DeFord is one of them. His wife, Lila, quarantined at home.

My first reaction … was simply to give thanks and praise to the Lord, our Healer. Rev. DeFord and his wife, having tested positive for Coronavirus, journeyed through an emotional and spiritual storm, physically separated from one another but, I believe, still one in spirit.

Rev DeFord laid unresponsive for weeks in the ICU at the University of Maryland Charles Regional Medical Center, while his wife quarantined at home, under the care of their son. Enduring her own symptoms, Mrs. DeFord must have been devastated by her husband's condition and the passing of her mother, who had been hospitalized early on.

In response to the ceaseless prayers of the righteous, the Lord intervened: Mrs. DeFord recovered and emerged from quarantine in time to meet her husband when he was discharged from the hospital to a rehabilitation facility. The Lord raised him up, sound in mind, body, and spirit. This is nothing short of a miracle.

—Sandra E. Smith

**Pastor Tillett, Senior Pastor, Asbury-Broadneck UMC, Annapolis, MD, wrote:**

Rev. George and Lila DeFord are, to me, among the most beloved colleagues in ministry I have in the Baltimore-Washington Conference. I followed George at Mt. Zion UMC in Baltimore, MD in 1996. Over the years, we became trusted colleagues and friends. I was extremely concerned when I heard that George and his household had taken ill. His late mother-in-law was in her 90s, and he and Lila are at retirement age. To hear that COVID had struck the entire family was devastating.

We lifted up the entire family on our daily prayer call at Asbury Broadneck and besought the Lord to keep and heal Lila and to bring George out of his lengthy intubation and hospitalization and then through the grueling rehab. We had a chance to speak, and George relayed his journey to me. I wouldn't wish it on anyone, but I am grateful that their faith and prayers, with God's help, brought them through. They are now examples and heralds to other colleagues and members of our conference who might have thought the virus wasn't real or 'not serious'. Anything that requires almost three weeks of intubation is beyond serious!

We continue to pray for their healing and restoration and hope this memoir will jar others out of their denial or complacency! To God be the glory for the things He has done!

—Pastor T

\* \* \*

# FRIENDS AND MORGAN STATE UNIVERSITY ALUMNI COLLEAGUES

**Shelley L., friend and registered nurse and supervisor, expressed:**
I felt helpless, torn, devastated. It's my nature to take care of people. It's what God designed me for, and to not be able to physically be there and care for two people who mean so much to my family, without endangering myself and risk exposing my household, left me with those feelings. No one could have clinically/medically cared for them as I would have; and to not be a part of the healthcare team left me worried sick that they would miss something and ... at that point I turned to God. He loves you both much more than I ... than us ... putting mine, Alex, Lexy and Jasper's complete faith in Him—that He would heal and make both of them whole ... praying daily—separately and together as a family ... we kept faith in the Lord...and when Lila came home ... and I heard the strength in her voice through the weakness ... my heart soared ... and then the video of Rev leaving the hospital ... I exhaled ... dropped to my knees where I stood and thanked Him ... and we continue to thank Him for keeping both of them here for their family and for mine.
—SHELLEY L.

**Jasper, husband of Shelley and father of Alex and Lexy, wrote:**
After having to leave a care package and mail outside your door, there was a hint that you guys were really not well. I would have to say that hearing of your Coronavirus infections personalized the pandemic

119

but it, also, allowed me to specify my prayers and put a name to the sickness that would devastate so many and was, now, threatening the great villagers who had positively impacted and nurtured my family for years.

—Jasper L.

**Alex, son of Jasper and former European professional basketball player, wrote:**

My relationship with the DeFords has been in cultivation since I was a young tyke. No matter how old I get, however, I can't shake the thought that they still see me as the first grader, who would come over to their home because I locked myself out of my own. Maybe I can't shake that thought because the stories from that time of my life are such a staple in our conversations when we have our annual summer lunch meetings, lunch meetings that have halted this year. I always cherished these opportunities to fellowship with the DeFords, seeing as though I'm usually only in the area for a couple of months out of the year. This year was different, though: not only due to lockdowns and the closure of businesses, but because the DeFords actually fell victim to the COVID-19 virus. This is when the magnitude of the pandemic started to resonate with me.

I was extremely worried when I heard that both Mr. George and Mrs. Lila DeFord had fallen ill with the COVID-19 virus. I saw statistics that placed them in the hyper-susceptible class of people when it came to the virus, and I wasn't sure what was going to happen. I prayed for them and hoped for the best. That was all that I could do. I thank God that they both made it through, and I know that the circumstances could have been otherwise, just as it has been for countless other people.

God has truly shown favor for the DeFords, and I am extremely grateful for that. I can't wait until we are able to meet up again and converse! —ALEX L.

**Lexy, the daughter of Jasper and Shelly L., wrote:**

Rev. and Mrs. DeFord, I hope you both feel better and that you stay safe throughout this uncertain time. I'm sorry to hear about Mrs. DeFord's mother and that you're both under the weather, but I am praying for your well-being, peace of mind, and continued encouragement. Things may be rough now, but everything works according to His will, and He won't abandon us (something I often need to be reminded of). 2 Chronicles 16:9 is one of my favorite verses, I find it comforting and encouraging when I feel down: "The eyes of the Lord search the whole earth in order to strengthen those whose hearts are fully committed to Him."

God bless you both, feel better, and I love you. —ALEXY, LEXY

**Dorothy Denise P., a long-time friend, succinctly wrote:**

I just started praying that God would restore both of them to health. Delmar (my son) was concerned, asking if the Reverend was going to be alright? And I was concerned about Lila, if something happened and the Reverend didn't pull through. That was a very emotional time for me. Because Lila and the Reverend mean so much to me. —DENISE

**Gwendolyn K., clergy wife and friend, wrote:**

Around Eastertime 2020, I was informed that Rev. George DeFord was hospitalized with the Coronavirus, that his wife, Lila, was at home with the virus, and that his mother-in-law had succumbed to the virus. I was devastated and reached out to Sister Lila DeFord. She informed me that she was fasting and praying for her husband's complete recovery and healing.

I told her that I would join her in fasting and praying and that I would invite my First Lady, Sister Stephanie West, to join us. We have been consistently connecting daily with additional prayer concerns, words of thanksgiving, and encouragement. We call ourselves PPW (Prayer and Praise Warriors).

To God be the Glory for hearing and answering our prayers.

Blessings!

—GWENDOLYN KENT

**Stephanie W., friend and First Lady, Westphalia UMC, Upper Marlboro, MD, wrote:**

I met Reverend DeFord by way of my husband, Timothy West, who is also a Pastor in the United Methodist Church. I knew of Rev. DeFord's wife because I remember hearing about how he introduced her as his wife and girlfriend. The real introduction of Mrs. DeFord came through Gwendolyn Kent, whom I call "Rev." Rev called me one day and asked if I would join her in fasting and praying for the DeFord family. That one call led to our strong bond as Prayer and Praise Warriors.

Reverend DeFord was in the hospital with COVID-19. The prognosis seemed somewhat dim for his recovery. Sister DeFord would give us the doctor's most recent reports on her husband via text messaging. Each report sent me to my knees in prayer, where the Spirit of the Living God would ask, "Whose report are you going to believe?"

I always had the same answer. I will believe the report of the Lord. He is a healer. I looked forward to sharing our words of encouragement and knowing we were connected in the spirit, bombarding heaven with our fervent prayers. I just knew Reverend DeFord was going to be released from the hospital to his wife, who is also his girlfriend. As we prayed, God's response at time felt like a rollercoaster—difficulties and turnarounds. We never gave up on God, and God proved faithful.

I remember the day so well when Sister Lila reported that Reverend DeFord asked for food. I went into praise and worship. I am getting excited all over again just thinking about that moment. Oh! The joy that flooded my soul! I ran to Tim's office to tell him the good news. I think I scared him because I was calling his name loudly and moving at the speed of lightning (smile). I am so glad we did not stop fasting, praying, trusting, or believing in our Savior. Our days of fasting and praying did multiple things—healed Reverend and Mrs. DeFord, gave me a new friend, and, most importantly, our conviction to believe that God answers prayer grew stronger. God healed! God made us friends and Prayer and Praise Warriors for life.

—STEPHANIE


**Thomas M. D. and Dr. Delores D., friends, classmates, and members of MSU Southern Maryland Alumni Chapter, wrote:**
We were overly concerned, but we knew that God was, and still is, in control. When Rev. DeFord was in the hospital, Mrs. DeFord (Lila) was the prayer warrior soliciting special focus for a return to good health.

*Jesus, I Trust in You* was the special ongoing feeling of prayer intentions.

The challenges of the pandemic and the celebration of life for loved ones have shown us the faith and belief demonstrated by the

Rev. and Lila. You are examples of his plan for ministry in the church, community, and family. Rev's commitment to the United Methodist Church, Morgan State University, local and national affiliations with the fraternal organizations are a credit to those of us who have been associated with him for many years. May God's plan for the DeFords be demonstrated in their life journey with faith, grace, and thanksgiving.
—THOMAS AND DELORES

**Karleen P., member of MSU Southern Maryland Alumni Chapter, described her reactions:**

Upon hearing about COVID-19, Reverend DeFord and Mrs. DeFord, it saddened me to learn that acquaintances of mine had been stricken with the virus. After hearing about the death of Mrs. DeFord's mother and the virus affecting them all around the same time, one could only imagine the difficult time they were experiencing. With Rev. DeFord being hospitalized miles away from home and Mrs. DeFord recovering at home in Southern Maryland, I thought, what can anyone say or do but pray that they both get well, and their health and strength be restored.
—KARLEEN P.

**Jocelyn M., member of MSU Southern Maryland Alumni Chapter, gave a succinct comment:**

When I found out Mrs. DeFord's mother transitioned and Rev. DeFord was in ICU recovering from COVID-19, I knew in my heart he might retire. Rev. DeFord served the Lord over these many years, faithfully, tirelessly, and lovingly.
—JOCELYN M.

**Cora M., friend, Morgan State University Alumnae, and member of St. Paul UMC, Oxon Hill, MD, wrote:**

May 19, 2020

Dear Lila,

Mere words are not ample! For you, I know this has been probably the most difficult time of your life.

Dealing with unknowns are trying times. This virus is ... what can I say? These are truly times that try men's souls. Thomas Paine wrote this in his *The American Crisis* during the American Revolution-1776—1783. How true it is today.

Losing your mom, then your husband's ordeal—what an ordeal!

Prayer is the answer to everything. A lot of prayers were and are still being prayed among the St. Paul Family. Many people have asked me for "Rev". They know Vera and I are friends; she is a member of his church. We all remember your time there with us.

It was a total impact, learning he had the virus. What a relief upon learning he opened his eyes, off the ventilator, later hungry. Best news—eating and feeding himself. Glory to God, who is in our lives and never leaves us!

I witnessed his departure from the hospital. What a wonderful, remarkable sight as the medical team lined the hall applauding another of God's miracles.

The most beautiful of all was the family at the end being able to give him a hug, your being able to give the love of your life a hug and a kiss after so much uncertainty. ONLY GOD!!

I pray that he is regaining his strength and will come home with you sooner than expected.

Stay safe and take care of yourself. Love,

—CORA M.

**Patient Liaison Intensive Care Unit, Charles Regional Medical Center, Karen P., RN, serving as patient liaison, shared:**

I was happy to hear Mr. DeFord's voice. He made my day, and I am filled with tears and thankful that he's doing well. I believe he was one of the first persons who recovered from the virus. I was praying for him. He was a miracle.

—Karen

## CHAPTER 5

# EXPRESSIONS OF ENCOURAGEMENT AND SYMPATHY

"Therefore, encourage one another with these words"
(1 Thessalonians 4:8)

The journey through the COVID-19 illness was emotionally challenging for my wife and me. While both Mother Margaret (my mother-in-law) and I were hospitalized in ICU, my wife was in quarantine at home. My Mother-in-law transitioned in the ICU due to the virus, and the entire family was under a tremendous amount of grief and stress. It was helpful to know that we were not alone in this struggle of sickness and death. There was a tremendous amount of compassion and empathy for our family. The various expressions of care and concern came from church members, friends, and social groups that gave words of encouragement and sympathy and offered to cut the grass and grocery shop for us. To illustrate the expressions of encouragement and sympathy, we selected cards, categorized them, and presented the written comments from church members, classmates, clergy, fraternity members, and friends. Additionally, devotional books, flowers, fruit baskets, and monetary gifts were sent to us by members of other congregations.

***The following sentiments—expressions of sympathy—were delivered to us from members of churches:***

Lila,

Our deepest sympathy and love,

Audrey, Roland, & Keisha

\* \* \*

4.14.20

Dear Sister DeFord,

We pray you have peace and comfort during this difficult time. We looked to God, too, and in Revelation 21:4, He promised to wipe away every tear. In the meantime, we love you and miss you and pray God's blessing upon Pastor DeFord.

Love you all much!

Pete and Mildred

(Staff Parish Chair and Member, Smith Chapel United Methodist)

\* \* \*

Dear Reverend and Mrs. DeFord,

Love you!!!

Your Smith Chapel Church Family

\* \* \*

Reverend and Mrs. DeFord,

Mother McRae was such a beautiful person. We will always remember her words of encouragement, glowing smile, and lovely sense of humor. May the Lord continue to comfort you.

Love You All,

Dorothy, Saint Gail, and Frost

(Members, Smith Chapel United Methodist Church)

\* \* \*

Mrs. DeFord,

I am sending my sincerest condolences, love, and comfort to you in the loss of your mom. Please know I love you and have been thinking about you too! I have been calling you, but no answer and I did not leave a message. I pray that Rev. DeFord (my buddy) and your sister are getting well, too! But I want you to get well soon! And know you are in my prayers now and always. Please take care and tell Rev "Hello," for me and Merton.

Love and Hugs,

Kathy M.

(Member, Metropolitan United Methodist Church)

PS: Tell Rev., get well soon, too, and stay strong!

\* \* \*

Hello Lila,

I'm happy to hear from you always. I love getting notes from you. I am grateful for knowing you and your mother. Time spent with the two of you will always be time I will not forget.

Bless You,

Iretha

\* \* \*

April 24, 2020

Mrs. DeFord

Just sending a little note letting you know I am praying and thinking about you and your family.

I really miss you and Rev so very much. May God continue to bless and heal you. It's not very much I can do presently except pray—but just know, I will be getting with you as soon as I can to do more!

Love and Prayers,

Barbara W.

PS: Love to Rev. & All

(Staff Parish Chair and Member, Smith Chapel United Methodist Church)

\* \* \*

Dear Reverend and Mrs. DeFord,

Love you!!!

Your Smith Chapel Church Family

\* \* \*

Mrs. DeFord, Reverend, and Family,

Mother McRae was such a beautiful person. We will always remember her words of encouragement, glowing smile, and lovely sense of humor. May the Lord continue to comfort you.

Love You All,

Dorothy, Saint Gail, and Frost

(Members, Smith Chapel United Methodist Church)

\* \* \*

Rev. and Mrs. DeFord,

We share your pain and are so very, very sorry for your loss. I was always inspired by your

Mother and her beauty.

Sincerely,

Mildred, Karlton, Keith, Kristi, Joel, and the girls (Betty and Aster)

We are here for you!

(Members of Metropolitan United Methodist Church)

\* \* \*

Rev. and Mrs. DeFord,

Know that you are all in our prayers! Thinking of you during this difficult time.

Love,

Patti and Ricky F. (Members of Pisgah United Methodist Church)

\* \* \*

April 30, 2020

Dear Lila,

My heart and love go but to you, at this time. Losing your Mother is the most difficult time in life. As the years go by, the memory of the beautiful care you gave her will help to heal.

All my family and friends are praying for you and Rev. If there is anything I can do, please call. You are both especially important to me and the Johnsons and Ebenezer.

Peace and Love,

Beverly (Member of Ebenezer United Methodist Church, DC)

\* \* \*

Dear Mrs. DeFord and Family,

Extending my deepest sympathy to you and the family.

God Bless,

Connie S. (Shiloh United Methodist Church)

\* \* \*

Dear Reverend and Mrs. DeFord,

I want to give you my deepest sorrow and sympathy on the passing of your mother, Mrs. McRae. May God's hope and love surround the both of you.

God Bless both of you,

C. Y. Davis

(Member of Ebenezer UMC, Washington, D.C.)

\* \* \*

Dear Lila,

Love and Prayers,

Marsha & Jimmy

(Members of Ebenezer United Methodist Church, DC)

\* \* \*

Dear Mrs. DeFord,

Love,

Millie H.

(Saint Mary's Star of the Sea Catholic Church)

* * *

Dear Reverend and Mrs. DeFord,

Prayers and God's Blessings.

Love,

Girard and Edith

(Members of Metropolitan United Methodist Church)

**The next group of cards focuses on encouragement to get well:**
April 27, 2020

Mrs. DeFord,

Thinking of you. To say how much you and Rev. DeFord are missed and we love you both very much. The Robertson and Bowman Family are praying for healing in Jesus' name!

Love,

Luther, Almalita, and Family

* * *

May 2, 2020

Dear Sister, DeFord,

Just dropping a note to let you know we continue to pray for you and Pastor DeFord for complete healing. We were so happy to hear that you and Pastor are steadily recovering.

May God continue to bless you and give you strength!!

Much Love,

Bob and Judy E.

(Members of Grace United Methodist Church, Fort Washington)

* * *

Rev. and Mrs. DeFord,

I will be talking to you real soon. I am praying for all of you. May God bless you … When this virus is on the really down-side, I will call and prepare "something" for you.

Love,

Barbara and Jarriett

(Members, Smith Chapel United Methodist Church and Saint Mary Star of the Sea Catholic Church)

PS: I didn't send the card to the hospital; I hope you are home real soon.

* * *

May 5, 2020

Dear Mrs. DeFord,

God is Good!

I am happy to know Rev is doing better—I am praying for your continued health and support for him also. Just know, I will be in prayer always for you and your family. Please give my love to your entire family.

Love always,

Barbara

(Member, Smith Chapel United Methodist Church)

PS: I will be sending cards, as I told Rev. DeFord one day, "Old folks don't text." (Smile)

* * *

May 2020

To The DeFords

Recuperation takes time. Don't rush yourself, rest as much as you can, heal, and I am sure you'll be feeling better soon.

Thinking of you Both,

Yvonne Marbray

(Member of Metropolitan United Methodist Church, Indian Head)

* * *

May 19, 2020

Rev. and Mrs. DeFord

Praying for You.

With much love,

Dorothy M.

(Member, Pisgah UMC, La Plata, MD)

\* \* \*

Dear Rev. and Mrs. DeFord,

Please know that I am praying for your healing and speedy recovery.

Blessings,

Eva S. Chesley

(Member of Metropolitan UMC, Indian Head, MD)

\* \* \*

May 2020

Dear Rev and Mrs. DeFord,

We are keeping you in prayer! Hold on to God's Word to encourage and strengthen you.

Peace and Blessings,

Anita, Norman and Family

\* \* \*

May 20, 2020

Dear Rev. and Mrs. DeFord,

We are so thankful to know Rev. DeFord has been released from the hospital. What a Blessing!! Prayers have been answered. We continue to pray for your return to good health.

God Bless,

Bob and Judy E.

(Members of Grace United Methodist Church, Fort Washington)

\* \* \*

June 6, 2020

Dear Rev. and Mrs. DeFord,

So amazingly happy to know Rev. is home and improving every day. What a Blessing!

May God continue to bless and strengthen you both. Enjoy your second retirement.

Much Love,

Judy E.

(Member of Grace United Methodist Church, Fort Washington)

\* \* \*

Dear Rev.,

Keeping you in prayer.

Love you,

Audrey

(Member of Smith Chapel United Methodist Church)

* * *

Dear Rev. and Mrs. DeFord,

I am sending this letter to share that my Prayers are with both of you. I must admit that I had purchased a Get-Well Card, however … the signature was a Big Mess. LOL. Rev. DeFord, I have learned that "LIFE IS BEAUTIFUL" and when you are thrown a LEMON, get yourself a pitcher, some sugar, and MAKE yourself some Lemonade. Inside: Praying that your recovery is speedy and that the Lord will comfort you as you heal.

Blessings, Healing, Grace, and Love to both of you,

Rosetta D.

(Grace United Methodist Church)

PS: Enjoy *Jesus Calling Morning & Evening* by Sarah Young

* * *

Rev. DeFord,

Get well soon!

Vera,

(Lay Leader, Smith Chapel United Methodist Church)

\* \* \*

Pastor DeFord,

Please take care of yourself,

The Broomes

(Members of Indian Head United Methodist Church)

\* \* \*

Rev. and Mrs. DeFord,

We are praying for your continued healing and know that we are here for you. We love you both and miss you.

The Masons,

Dorothy, David, Saint Gail, Frost, Mark

(Members of Smith Chapel United Methodist Church)

\* \* \*

Rev. and Mrs. Lila,

You are in my prayers.

Yours in Christ,

Mildred and Family

We are more than a conqueror through Him who loved us. (Romans 8:37 NIV)

\* \* \*

Rev. and Mrs. DeFord,

3 John 1:2 Dear Friends,

I pray that you may enjoy good health and that all may go well with you, even as your soul is getting along well.

May God Bless You Always, Love,

Pete and Mildred

(Members, Smith Chapel United Methodist Church)

\* \* \*

Dear Pastor DeFord,

Thank God for answered prayers.

Peace and Love and Much Blessings,

M. H. D.

\* \* \*

Dear Dr. DeFord,

I am so happy you are feeling better. God is wonderful!!

Rothel D.T. C.

(Saint Paul United Methodist Church, Oxon Hill)

* * *

Dear Rev.,

It was wonderful news to hear you have made great progress. We pray you will soon have a complete recovery.

Blessings and Love always,

Maxine and George S.

(Saint Mark's United Methodist Church, Laurel)

* * *

Dear Rev. DeFord,

So glad you are feeling better and that you are on the mend!

We love you and pray for you each day!

God Bless You!

Marsha and Jimmy

(Members, Ebenezer United Methodist Church, Washington D.C.)

* * *

Dear Rev. and Lila DeFord,

Praying for you both.

With Love,

Gordon and Ann G.

(Members, Saint Mark's United Methodist Church, Laurel)

\* \* \*

Dear Rev. DeFord,

Feel better soon!

Blessings and Peace,

Ms. Mil and Family

(Members, Ebenezer United Methodist Church, Washington, D.C.)

\* \* \*

Rev.,

Get well soon!

Peace and Grace,

Ryan, Kia, and Briana

(Members, Smith Chapel United Methodist Church)

\* \* \*

Dearest Rev. and Mrs. DeFord,

We placed you in God's care in our prayers and He blessed you both with His healing touch. We are so very grateful to God for taking care of you and your family during this pandemic. May He continue to bless you both with strength, peace, and even joy.

Love,

Anthony and Patricia L.

(Members, Grace United Methodist Church, Fort Washington)

* * *

Dear Rev. DeFord,

I am one of your former School of Christian Growth class members, "Praying with the Scriptures."

God Bless you and Mrs. DeFord,

Mrs. Gertrude W.

(Member, Nash United Methodist Church, Washington, D.C.)

* * *

Rev. Dr. and Mrs. DeFord,

Our thoughts and prayers are with you all, and we wish you both, a speedy recovery!

Love,

Miss Helen's, Girls and Boys: Romaine, Sharon, Patsy, Shelly, Garrett, and Bobby, (Members, Metropolitan United Methodist Church)

PS: We miss you all. Forgive the lateness of this card. May God Bless you!

* * *

Dr. DeFord,

Keeping you close in thought.

(The Tribe of Naphtali of Grace United Methodist Church)

* * *

Dear Rev. and Mrs. DeFord,

We are praying constantly for your comfort and healing. Words cannot adequately express how much we love you and care about you at this very difficult time.

Please know that we're here for you and pray for God's comfort and peace for you and your family.

Much Love,

Bob and Judy E.

(Members, Grace United Methodist Church, Fort Washington, MD)

* * *

Warmest thoughts and prayers are sent your way today.

I'm hoping soon you will be as good as new.

Joan K. M. and Family

(Members, Metropolitan United Methodist Church, Indian Head, MD)

\* \* \*

Dear Rev. and Mrs. DeFord,

Praising Him for His continued faithfulness toward us!

Peace and Blessings,

Sis. Sharon C-J

(Grace United Methodist Church, Fort Washington, MD)

\* \* \*

We miss you!

God bless,

Audrey and Roland

(Members, Smith Chapel United Methodist Church, La Plata, MD)

\* \* \*

Our prayers are with you and your family.

Thomas and Evelyn D.

(Members, Metropolitan UMC, Indian Head, MD)

* * *

Continue to look to the Lord!!

With Love,

Kia, Ryan and Briana

(Members, Smith Chapel UMC, La Plata, MD)

* * *

Rev. and Mrs. DeFord,

When we pray for healing, our prayers will be heard, and if it is your will, God, our bodies will be whole again.

As hard as it is to do, we must let go and let God take over and know that His love for all His children is eternal, steadfast, and true.

Love,

Mrs. Nancy

PS: I Love and miss you both very much. God be with you always.

(Member, Smith Chapel UMC, La Plata, MD)

* * *

I thank God for your recoveries, and may God continue to keep you both in His loving care.

Sincerely,

Willette W.

(Member, Grace UMC, Fort Washington, MD)

* * *

Dear Rev. DeFord,

We were very happy to learn you are making real progress. We pray you will be back to your old self soon.

Blessings and Love,

Maxine and George S.

(Members, Saint Mark's UMC, Laurel, MD)

* * *

Dear Mrs. DeFord,

I pray that the Lord will watch over you and your family and keep you in His care. The Lord is still on the throne.

Peace, Love, and Blessings,

M. H. D.

PS: I hope this poem (I Can't Remember) will put a smile on your face.

(Member, Ebenezer UMC, Washington, D.C.)

\* \* \*

Dear Rev. and Mrs. DeFord,

You both are a wonderful expression of God's love in this world. I will always be grateful for the care and concern that you have shown for me and for my family, no just now in a difficult time but over the years.

"Thank You" are just a few simple words, but know that they come from my heart.

With much love and forever grateful,

Rachel, Kyle and Olivia J.

(Members, Smith Chapel UMC, La Plata, MD)

\* \* \*

Rev. DeFord,
Hope you are feeling better today!

Vera

PS: Wear this mask with the UM Pride!

(Lay Leader, Smith Chapel UMC, La Plata, MD)

**The next group of cards came from clergy colleagues, staff members of the judicatory, and the spouse of a deceased episcopal leader:**

May 9, 2020

Dear George,

So glad to hear that you are out of the hospital. My daughter—who is a nurse practitioner at the University of Maryland-St. Joseph—tells me this is a really nasty staph.

God bless you and all your family.

City Forever!

Emora B.

(High School Chum and Retired Clergy Baltimore-Washington Conference)

\* \* \*

Dear Rev., DeFord,

Thinking of you and praying for your recovery.

Pastor Cindy and Shiloh Congregation

\* \* \*

Thinking of you …

Obie and Authuree

(Retired Clergy Members, Baltimore-Washington Conference)

\* \* \*

May 11, 2020

Dear Friends,

Sending daily prayers for your continued recovery. God is Good, God is our Help in every need, God cares for us and will bring us health and healing.

"God's Love is Healing,

God's Love renews, makes us whole,

Love will Restore You!" (An original Haiku Poem)

Blessings! Peace and Hope,

Phyllis May and Bishop May's Spirit

(Wife of late former Episcopal leader, the Baltimore-Washington Conference)

\* \* \*

Sending good healthy wishes your way!

The Washington East District of the Baltimore-Washington Conference

Rev. Dr. Johnsie W. Cogman and Staff

(District Superintendent)

\* \* \*

Thanking God for what He has already done and praying for your full recovery!

Blessings,

Rev. Stella T. and Family

(Retired Clergy, BWC)

* * *

Dear George,

Continuing to keep you and Mrs. DeFord in our prayers for a full recovery.

Mark V. and Ebenezer UMC

(Pastor, Lanham, MD)

* * *

Dear Dr. DeFord and Miss Lila,

First, praise The Lord Almighty for your healing!

I had no idea of the battle you have faced, the season you have endured. But just know I am truly grateful that God is seeing you through.

It is my prayer that God continues to release healing and that you continue to be strengthened in both body and spirit. And that you are loved, thought of, and prayed for.

Pat and Ed A.

(Pastor and Husband)

\* \* \*

Dear Rev. DeFord,

The Baltimore-Washington Conference is glad to hear that you are on the mend.

Continued prayers of strength and good health are being said for you.

Benefits Office BWC UMC

Francess T. and Karen C.

\* \* \*

Dr. and Mrs. DeFord,

You are living proof that God is still in the healing business.

Know that you are in my thoughts and prayers. May God's love surround you as God's grace sustains you.

I love you so much!

Blessings,

Jacob C.

(Associate Pastor, Christ Church UMC, Kentucky)

\* \* \*

God be with You,

Rev. and Mrs. Victor O. J.

(Retired Pastor, BWC UMC)

* * *

With the Love of Christ.

The Metropolitan UMC Family,

Rev. Darryl M. and Michelle M-M.

(Pastor and First Lady, Indian Head, MD)

* * *

Thinking of you,

Elder Bobby S. and Mother Patricia S.

* * *

For you, I am praying.

Yours in Christ,

Elder Mary F. H.

* * *

**The next group of cards comes from members of the Morgan State University Southern Maryland Alumni Chapter (MSUSMAC) and the members of the graduating Class 1967, a/k/a "Soulful Centennials":**

Sorry for your loss,

Sylvia P.

(Class '67 and MSUSMAC)

* * *

With Sympathy,

Morgan State University Southern Maryland Alumni Chapter

* * *

From Both of Us,

Thomas and Delores D.

(Class '67 and MSUSMAC)

* * *

With Sympathy,

Gloria E. S.

(MSUSMAC)

* * *

May your strength be renewed each day. Just as the sun rises, Our Lord, the <u>SON,</u> renews and heals our bodies, souls, and spirits.

Patricia F.

(MSUSMAC)

\* \* \*

Wishing you comfort,

Victor and Bettie W.

(MSUSMAC)

\* \* \*

Hope you are up and about soon,

Sylvia P.

(Class '67 and MSUSMAC)

\* \* \*

Rev. DeFord,

Get Well Soon!

Your MSUSMAC colleagues and friends. Take care of yourself in these trying times.

All the best.

\* \* \*

Please get well soon!

Sincerely,

Vera M.

(MSUSMAC)

\* \* \*

Dear George,

Praying for you.

Faithfully and prayerfully yours,

Warren H.

(Class '67 and Friends of the Chapel)

\* \* \*

Classmate George,

God's comfort and strength!

Soulful Centennial Classmate,

Tamara G.

(Class '67)

\* \* \*

June 6, 2020

Dear George,

While too many years have gone by since being in one another's company—as a fellow MSU Classmate, my wife, Janet, and I wish you all the best!

R. Lance (Reggie) and Janet L. G.

(Class '67)

* * *

George,

I was so sorry to hear that you have been suffering from COVID-19. My prayers are for you to have a complete recovery!

Sincerely,

Joyce H. S.

(Class '67)

* * *

George,

Wishing you … feel better and stronger tomorrow.

Otis M.

(Class '67)

* * *

**Several cards are from my Fraternity Brothers of
Phi Beta Sigma, Inc. :**

Brother Rev. DeFord,

Our thoughts are with you, and we are all praying for a full recovery
for you and First Lady DeFord.

From your brothers at the Zeta Chi Sigma Chapter of Phi Beta
Sigma Fraternity, Inc.

\* \* \*

Brother and Mrs. DeFord,

Please know that we are here for you if you need anything. Our
prayers for healing and strength are with you.

Brother Benjamin and Shelia D.

(Member, FBS, ZCS)

\* \* \*

**The remaining cards come from friends who expressed their
sorrow for the loss of Mother McRae and hope for our recovery
from COVID-19:**

You all have been like family more than know; I am going to miss
her so much. Time and Jesus heal all pain.

Bless you, with every ounce of strength that I have,

Ron and Wendy

PS: You were supposed to be my stepdaughter. (Smile)

When I got the news of what you are going through, I cried like a baby. Hoping that my tears could help share some of your pain. We are going to ride out this storm right beside you 'til Jesus decides to calm the sea. The least little thing I could do to help, please do not hesitate to call. Love you so much,

Ron and Wendy

\* \* \*

Lila,

Know that our hearts and prayers are with you and Rev. DeFord at this time. I am sorry we could not make the service, but we were there in spirit. May you both continue to heal and get stronger.

Love,

Shelly, Jasper, and Kids

\* \* \*

Dear Ms. Lila,

With deepest sympathy,

Love you,

Lenora

\* \* \*

Dear Mrs. DeFord,

With sympathy,

Daniel Y. and Family

\* \* \*

Dear Rev. DeFord,

I have added your name to a special enrollment under the special patronage of Our Lady of Lourdes for Masses of Healing for one full year at the Sacred Grotto in Lourdes, France, and at the National Shrine of Our Lady of the Snows in Belleville, Illinois. Get well soon and feel better.

Sincerely,

Violet S.

(Former Secretary)

\* \* \*

Lila,

I was sorry to hear that your mother passed away. I hope that all is well with you. May God bless and keep you!

Delinda

\* \* \*

George,

I was so excited when Vincent told me that you had been released from the hospital. My prayers are with you daily.

Blessings,

Delinda

(Cousin)

* * *

Lila,

Love,

Denise and Delmar

* * *

Rev. DeFord,

I am continuing to pray for your healing.

Much love,

Beverly S. M.

* * *

Rev.

Thank the Lord you made it!

Love,

Ron and Wendy

\* \* \*

Also, a plethora of emails, telephone calls, and text messages came to Lila and Dante, who screened many of the communications while my wife was sick. Several of my fraternity brothers spoke with Lila by phone, in particular Brother Willie Harrison, who volunteered to have fraternity members cut our grass and shop for her during her quarantine. Brother Gerard M., who works in an ICU in a nearby northern Virginia hospital as a respiratory therapist, explained to my wife the type of procedure employed while I was on the ventilator, and most likely what my situation was. He encouraged Lila.

Clergy colleagues called during my hospitalization and upon my return home. Many promised to pray for our healing and have their intercessory prayer groups to do likewise. In addition, former members and students from Christian Growth classes called to let my family know that we were in their prayers.

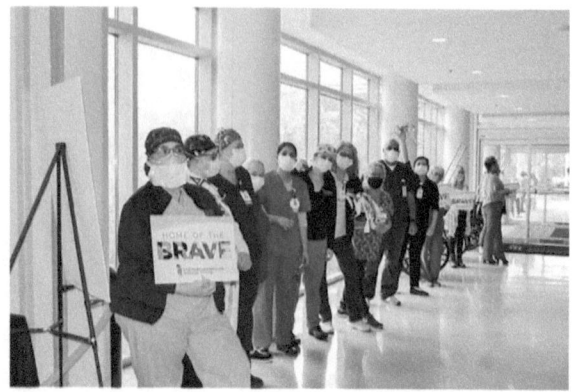

In LaPlata, Maryland, the University of Maryland Charles Regional Medical Center's healthcare team awaits my arrival in its hallway to celebrate my medical discharge. I left there, headed to a Rehabilitation Center in Baltimore.

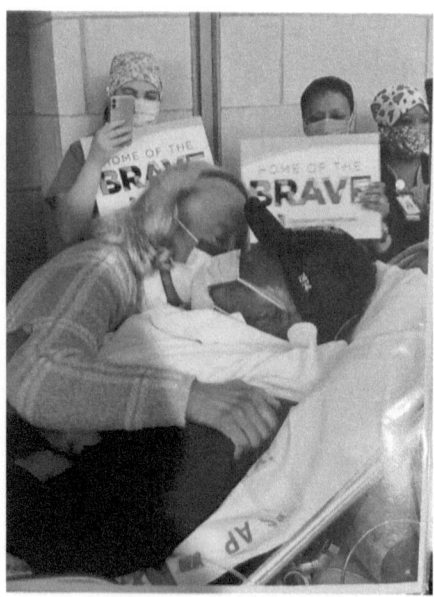

My wife, Lila, embraces me upon my medical center discharge, while the ICU team looks on.

Members of the ICU team from the University of Maryland Charles Regional Medical Center pose for a picture with my wife, Lila, after I left the medical center on my way to a rehab in Baltimore, MD.

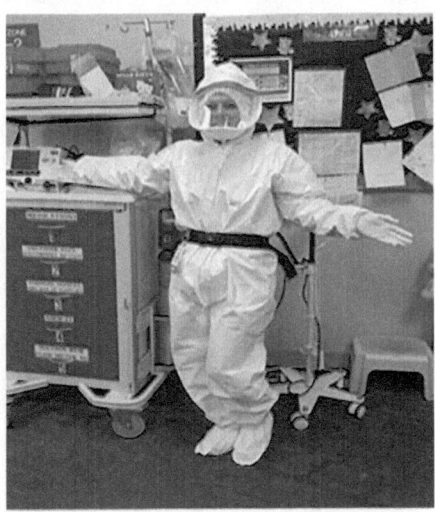

An ICU caregiver at the Univ. of MD Charles Regional Medical Center, in full Personal Protective Equipment (PPE), needed to keep staff members safe while fighting COVID-19. A caregiver, dressed in PPE, would possibly be the last person a dying COVID-19 patient saw. During the early days of the virus, family members were not allowed in the hospital.

The Prayer and Praise Warriors (PPW) of Westphalia Christian Community Church, a UMC congregation in Upper Marlboro, MD. (L) Mrs. Gwendolyn Kent, (Center) First Lady Mrs. Stephanie West, and (R) my wife, Mrs. Lila A. DeFord. These ladies banded together to pray for my recovery. Photo Credit: Dwight Coleman

The current 2025 Prayer and Praise Warriors (PPW) at Westphalia Christian Community Church in Upper Marlboro, MD. (L) Mrs. Gwendolyn Kent, (Center) First Lady Mrs. Stephanie West, (R) Mrs. Lila A. DeFord, and (on the end) Mrs. Johanna Coleman. These dedicated ladies are still praying for the sick and the shut-in. Photo Credit: Dwight Coleman

(L-R) Mary Hannah, VP, Population Health and Case Management; Rev. Dr. George F. DeFord and Mrs. Lila A. DeFord; and Teri White, Transitional Nurse Navigator. Both Hannah and White are on staff at the University of MD Charles Regional Medical Center in LaPlata, MD. They played pivotal roles in Rev. DeFord's 2020 hard-fought battle with COVID-19 and still remember him today. This photo was taken in June 2025.

# CHAPTER 6

# REFLECTION

"O Lord, my God, I cried unto thee, and thou hast
healed me … thou hast brought up my soul
from the grave; thou hast kept me alive "
(Psalm 30: 2-3 KJV)

L ila and I take a retrospective view of our experiences with the deadly
contagious Coronavirus described by a colleague of mine as a nasty
staph infection (staphylococcus bacteria, commonly found on the
skin or in the nose). We view our illness and recovery through the lens
of the Holy Bible, which contains a number of miraculous healing
episodes in both the Old and New Testaments. The Old Testament
character King David suffered a grave illness from which he received
healing and praised God for his recovery. Significantly, David declared,
" thou have kept me alive" (Psalm.30:3b KJV). We echo the psalmist's
declaration when thinking back over our sickness because of COVID-19
and recovery from the same due to the mercy of Almighty God, who
kept us alive. In the New Testament, especially in the gospels, there are

twenty-nine healing miracles, for example, the revival from death of a twelve-year-old girl and the healing of blind Bartimaeus (Mark 5:21-43; Luke 8:49-56; Mark 10:46-52). Each pointing to God's faithfulness to heal and keep humankind alive.

Nevertheless, the New Testament, while having life-giving and healing miracle narratives, has troubling life-threatening accounts. The Coronavirus has an apocalyptic feature similar to the account recorded in The Revelation to John. The apostle John recorded the vision of Seven Seals in which the fourth seal pertained to a pale green horse with the rider Death, and Hades that followed. The said rider and its compatriot exercised authority over a quarter of the earth, where they caused death with sword, famine, and pestilence, and by wild animals of the earth (Rev. 6:8). Some interpret the current pandemic in connection with the vision of the apostle of the revealed hidden message. Further, I have been in conversations with persons who are of an eschatological opinion that the Coronavirus is indicative that the end-time is now.

Our initial experiences during early spring 2020 were Jobian. That is to say, a series of unexpected calamities and health problems occurred, such as reported in the Old Testament Book of Job (Job 1:13-22). Mother fell one night and broke her hip, which required immediate hip surgery. Dre, our oldest son, suffered an extremely low white blood count, necessitating his hospitalization and quarantining for a week. Also, Lila fainted, hitting her head on the sharp edge of the armoire, causing a deep gash that required thirteen staples to close the wound. Mother suffered a stroke along with contracting the Coronavirus. Shortly thereafter, we became positive with COVID-19, which required different treatment modalities: Lila quarantined at home for two weeks while I remained in the hospital for thirty days, including fifteen days on a ventilator. Mother succumbed to the deadly virus on April 10,

2020, at 5 p.m., while I was close to death's door. Meanwhile, my wife recovered and became my intercessor along with other prayer partners. Although our problems mounted, we had compassionate, empathetic, and supportive family, church members, and friends to help us through the tumultuous times.

James, the uterine brother of our Lord, writes concerning The Prayer of Faith. He says, " and pray for one another, so that you may be healed. The prayer of the righteous is powerful and effective" (James 5:16b). The members of Smith Chapel United Methodist Church's Intercessory Prayer Team, along with the Prayer Praise Warriors (PPW), who are clergy spouses, former members, family, friends, and Dante bombarded heaven with prayer petitions for our healing. Along with the prayers, the intercessors practiced the spiritual discipline of fasting. Fasting and prayer are powerful and effective! I am convinced that the said practices were beneficial to my healing and recovery.

I am often reminded of Hezekiah's miraculous recovery from the illness of infectious boils as recorded in 1 Kings 20:1-11, 2 Chronicles 32:24-26 and Isaiah 38. King Hezekiah upon receiving word from the prophet Isaiah that death was imminent, he turned toward a wall and tearfully prayed to God to spare his life. God recanted God's will and directed the prophet to inform the king of an additional fifteen years of life. God heard the prayer of Hezekiah.

In light of Hezekiah's prayer to God for healing and his subsequent recovery, our situation spiritually gelled together. Lila received healing and I eventually opened my eyes on the weekend of April 26th.

**Excursus**: This is significant for me because on April 26, 1976 at 7 a.m. I surrendered my life to Christ as my Lord and Savior while in fervent prayer in my recreation room. I shared my spiritual experience with a seminary professor that interpreted my event as "cosmic consciousness". John Wesley, founder of the Methodist movement, cited his heart being strangely warmed on May 24, 1738, in the evening while in a meeting on Aldersgate Street in London; Wesley felt he trusted in Christ and Christ alone for salvation.

Also, Mrs. LaTisha Hall, an environmental service employee at the University of Maryland, Charles Regional Medical Center, frequently prayed over me and other ICU patients; she said, "Okay, DeFord, it is time to breathe on your own, in the name of Jesus."

Like Lazarus, I had my great awakening while called forth from the tomb of an induced coma.

I do not negate the professional work of the medical staff whose members are gifted, skilled, and well-trained in the medical arts and sciences. It is my opinion that they are the expressed manifestation of the hands of God's healing mercies. And I firmly believe that the intercessions of the prayer partners, in addition to fasting, coupled with the intensive work of the medical team, helped keep me alive. Moreover, my will to live mobilized my body's natural mechanisms of resistance to Coronavirus.[1] Cousins contends the will to live is not a theoretical abstraction but a reality with therapeutic characteristics.[2] Thus, the healing hands of the medical team members along with the prayers of the saints plus my will to live as did King Hezekiah and God's mercy allowed me to live. Thanks be to God!

The extended stay in the hospital as a bedridden patient weakened my leg muscles; thus, when my transfer occurred, the ambulance crew placed me on a gurney, securing me for the travel to Baltimore. At the rehabilitation center, I was designated as a fall-risk. The physical therapist focused on strengthening my legs while I maintained the erroneous attitude of being stronger than actually was the case. It would be subsequent to my return home that I accepted the truth: my legs were weak, and I had too much pride.

My rehabilitation center experience, in part, did not lend itself to ataraxy. I was not at my best or reflective of the presence of the *imago Christi*. Feeling alone and in a strange place did not help my attitude being calm, peaceful, or stop my yearning to be home with my family. Further, my innate reluctance to be a patient in a nursing home although on the rehabilitation side of the facility only complicated matters for me. I did not apply the teaching of the apostle Paul, who wrote: " for I have learned to be content with whatever I have" (Philippians 4:11b). What I had at that moment was residency in a rehabilitation center far away from home. There are certain instances during my stay at the rehabilitation center I wished could be rewritten, particularly with my attitude of being a boastful senescent athlete who does not need help. However, I have a keener insight as to the various stressors that contribute to militating against some of the employees' dispositions: not enough help, longer duty hours, the constant harangue of patients, and the deaths of patients while alone. Now, I have a greater admiration for the health care workers in nursing homes and rehabilitation centers.

The apostle John records the occasion of a disabled man who sat on a mat at the pool of Bethesda for thirty-eight years and was unable to receive the benefit of healing when the waters were troubled by an angel because others overstepped him and jumped in the water. Jesus questioned the man about his circumstances and desire to walk. Upon hearing the man's complaint, Jesus said, "Stand up, take your mat and walk." At once, the man was made well, and he took up his mat and began to walk (John 5:8, 9). I identify with the biblical character because of my inability to walk; yet, because of being away from the rehabilitation center and at home, where I could exercise daily, my attitude became positive as the strength in my legs increased and enabled me to go from the hallway inside the house to the outside driveway. From the driveway to the roadway of the cul de sac, to walking the community roadway two and one-half times, equivalent to slightly over a mile, I began to feel like myself again. The Lord does order our steps.

Also, the matter of speech impediment is not new; in fact, Quohelet said, " there is nothing new under the sun," (Ecclesiastes 1:9c). Jesus, according to Mark's gospel, performed a miraculous healing on a man who was deaf and had a speech impediment. "He took him aside in private, away from the crowd, and put his finger into his ears, and he spat and touched his tongue. Then looking up to heaven, he sighed and said to him, 'Ephphatha' that is, 'Be opened.' And immediately his ears were opened, his tongue was released, and he spoke plainly," says the gospel writer (Mark 7:33-35). I continue to pray and look for further healing as it relates to my memory and speech.

The apostle Paul in his first correspondence to the Corinthian church concerning unworthily receiving the sacrament of Holy Communion, says, "Let a man examine himself " (1 Corinthians 11: 28a). I find the passage of Holy Scripture appropriate for me. In a moment of self-examination, I asked myself, "What do you, George, take away from this experience?" Honestly, I struggle to carve words to express my feelings. Nevertheless, God is faithful to God's Word. While as of this time, four hundred thousand died, and yet God spared us to this moment. God is good, and all the time God is good!

I recently read a devotional that addressed the matter of hope while suffering. The meditation, based upon Lamentations 3:19-26, spoke to my spirit, especially with its prayer and thought for the day. I quote, "God who heals, help us to express our gratitude to you by offering our lives to you for your purposes. Use us for your glory. Amen."[3] The thought presented was, "I will share my story of God's faithfulness with someone today."[4] Hence, Lila and I share our experiences with the Coronavirus illness with hopes that someone will be encouraged despite the shadow of death cast by the deadly virus.

This experience of being miraculously healed from the coronavirus illness is not a hoax but a very sobering time for us, particularly in knowing that tomorrow is not promised. With the sudden demise of Mother Margaret while in the IUC with me and my unawareness of her transition, I could not have imagined such a day would happen. We all believed Mother would become a centenarian. The fabric of our family was traumatically torn. We still speak of Mother in the present.

I am especially grateful to God for "My Girlfriend and Wife who is One and the Same" who walked the dark valley of COVID-19 with me. Lila is an anointed woman of God and spiritually tenacious who agreed to walk with me on this journey (Amos 3:3). Well said by King Lemuel's mother, "A capable wife who can find? She is far more precious than jewels. The heart of her husband trusts in her, and he will have no lack of gain. She does him good, and not harm, all the days of her life" (Proverbs 31:10-12). In light of the Jobian calamities that came into our lives, we continue to hold each as very precious and thank God for the time and love we have together. Thanks be to God!

The Coronavirus is a Goliathan pandemic that can be defeated with the cooperation of all. Notwithstanding the political rhetoric in the atmosphere, the horrific numbers of deaths due to COVID-19 that surpass the fatalities of World War II, and the daily death totals equivalent to 9/11, there are means to conquer this insidious virus. To do this, it requires all to join together in utilizing the prescribed precautionary measures outlined by the health authorities, while allowing me to use a metaphorical approach.

The Old Testament (Hebrew Scriptures) has an account of the young shepherd David who confronts the Philistine giant Goliath. The young ruddy shepherd boy met the giant Goliath in a valley between the two opposing armies. David, unable to wear the battle gear of King Saul, found five smooth stones and put them into his shepherd's bag. Young David fearlessly met the giant and felled him with a stone in the center of the gigantic opponent's forehead. The giant fell face forward, and David decapitated him with his own (1 Samuel 17:40-54).

The coronavirus can be defeated with five smooth stones available to all of us. Here are the five smooth stones (practices):

Washing hands thoroughly for twenty seconds.

Wearing face covering.

Keeping social distancing.

Avoiding large crowds.

Receiving vaccinations.

Metaphorical stones serve as a means to save our lives! Our Creator God gave gifts, talents, and wisdom to those in the medical profession to apply them to those struck down by the vicissitudes of life, such as the Coronavirus infection. Notwithstanding the medical professionals' God-given unique graces and skills employed in conjunction with the spiritual disciplines of fasting and praying by others, God intervenes in mysterious ways to bring forth healing. The unexplainable action of the Divine working in human history is miraculous. For George DeFord, it was a miracle that caused me to live. In the words of David, the psalmist, said, "thou hast kept me alive," (Psalm 30:3). God kept me, and He didn't let go.

## CHAPTER 7

# ECHOES FROM THE DARK STORM

"He made darkness his covering around him, his canopy
thick clouds with water … The Lord also thundered in the
heavens, and the Most High uttered his voice"
(Psalm 18:11, 13)

The scientific community considers April 8, 2024, a significant date. A total solar eclipse occurred between 2-4 p.m. across certain areas of the United States from the southeastern region to the upper northeast. Millions of people gathered to see the cosmic event while equipping themselves with specially designed protective eyewear. The viewing public watched the moon pass in front of the sun, causing a complete block-out of the sun and total darkness for several minutes. The phenomenon was a rare occurrence that was a lifetime experience. However, the eclipse for me pointed back to a dark moment in my family's life. It is now five years, a quinquennium, since my wife and I suffered the COVID-19 infection and our family's 97-year-old matriarch succumbed to the deadly virus. We felt caught in our darkest hour while at the mercy of a ferocious storm.

I recall as a child when my late sister, Brenda, and I stayed with our maternal grandmother in a three-story row house in West Baltimore on the days when our mother worked. There was a storm on one occasion; I vividly remember our grandmother telling us to be quiet because the Lord was talking during the storm. Perhaps, our grandmother recalled from the Bible, "The voice of the Lord is powerful; the voice of the Lord is full of majesty ... The voice of the Lord flashes forth flames of fire" (Psalm 29:4, 7). What stood out in my mind was the clear echo of the thunder reverberating from the third floor of the stairwell. Brenda and I stayed quiet and covered our heads as we sheltered ourselves under the quilted covers on the makeshift beds of dining room chairs. Soon after, we were glad that the Lord stopped directly talking to us, but we continued to hear the echo of God's voice in a distant area of the city. We were afraid to go to the bathroom on the second floor because of the recurring echoes from the distant rumblings of thunder. As an adult, I recall the late Reverend Charles Albert Tindley, who wrote the hymn, *The Storm is Passing Over*. However, COVID-19 still lingers with us as variants, like echoes from a distant storm.

Referring to the COVID-19 Global Pandemic as a storm is a powerful metaphor. The pandemic devastated people worldwide. Many in our present multiple generations are not aware of the pandemic of 1919 that killed tens of thousands in America. Yet, the effects of the coronavirus pandemic continue as echoes from a violent storm, five years later.

The State of Maryland suffered 18,366 deaths due to COVID-19 as of March 11, 2025, among whom were 460 Charles countians as indicated by data from the State of Maryland's Open Portal. To recapitulate, in the month of April 2020, there were 10 deaths in Charles County, of whom my mother-in-law was among those statistics. I learned that I was among the first survivors of the deadly virus. My survival was celebrated on my discharge from the University of Maryland Charles Regional Medical Center, LaPlata, Maryland, on May 8, 2020. My discharge was publicized on local media and social media. Some of my former members of other congregations, whom I served, contacted my family to express their praise to God for "sparing Reverend."

My miraculous recovery was because of God's providential care and wisdom imparted to the medical teams of that illustrious Medical Center in LaPlata. Because of the healing mercy extended to me by God, an essential part of my daily devotions and scripture readings is the account of King Hezekiah's recovery and extension of life as recorded in 2 Kings 20: 1-11; 2 Chronicles 32: 24-26; and Isaiah 38. As I read the said passages of Holy Scripture, I give thanks to God for God's gracious and merciful kindness during that very dark and stormy time. Each day is a time for rejoicing (Psalm 118:24). An old saint many years ago said, "God is a good God!" I echo the same sentiments.

Looking back at those dark and stormy days in the spring of 2020, I discover that there are echoes. The metaphorical echoes are daggers of painful memories. The DeFord and Schofield families were forever changed because of the sudden death of our grand matriarch, Mother. While our family, like many others, was a victim of the coronavirus, we, too, experienced profound pain. It was not until I participated in a seminar sponsored by the Baltimore-Washington Conference of the United Methodist Church and conducted at Westphalia Christian Community Church in Upper Marlboro, MD, during the spring of 2024, that I learned and understood what truly happened. Dr. Debroah G. Haskins, licensed psychotherapist and lecturer, defined and unpacked the meaning of trauma. Our family not only experienced grief but also the associated trauma.

I learned, "trauma comes from the Greek and refers to things that can wound, hurt, or defeat a person … It will include death, perhaps the death of a child or significant member by pandemics … the traumatizing event is global or personal, its impact on individuals, families and communities can be profound."[1] So, with that understanding, while (dare I say) most people assume that the threat of this virus is over or at least no longer threatening, in actuality, the events of the COVID-19 Global Pandemic continue to be a profoundly devastating reverberation from the past. It still leaves its indelible markings on our lives.

I recognize the lingering trauma of COVID-19, as someone who suffers from some of COVID's long-term symptoms: fatigue, brain fog, dizziness, heart palpitations, and chest pains. I experienced fatigue and occasional dizziness several times after enthusiastic preaching; during the fall of 2024, not only did I feel fatigued and dizzy, but I also became nauseous and needed assistance from several lay members and ushers to leave the pulpit—most embarrassing. I was driven home by another layman and fraternity brother. Now, whenever I deliver a sermon, my wife ensures that one of our sons or two former church members will drive us home, given the possibility of my becoming overly fatigued resulting from preaching engagements.

During my hospitalization, when I had flashed moments of consciousness while in the ICU, as I mentioned earlier, I vaguely recalled the removal of a patient who had died. I believe I saw staff members in astronaut-like outfits pushing a gurney with a white zipper bag that I assumed held a body. That moment has stayed with me. It's my internal association—the dichotomy of my role as a pastor, witnessing such a thing along with its associated grief (many times over), intertwined with the struggle for my own life—in real time. It is the trauma that rumbled through my ailing body then and continues to resonate with me now.

Another traumatic event occurred after my discharge on May 8th, 2020, from the University of Maryland Charles Regional Medical Center. The Genesis Loch Raven Rehabilitation Facility was not a good experience for me. As a recapitulation, looking back, the event of my having a bad exchange with a night duty nurse periodically surfaces. And it surfaced in my mind how, many years ago, one of my senior members said, "Pastor, you got to watch them night nurses."

The night that I called for assistance to go to the bathroom, and what I perceived as an undue delay, caused me to take matters into my own hands and make the effort to get out of bed and go to the toilet. I recalled how, during the previous weekend, the physical therapist had shown me how to get out of bed on my own. Upon coming out of the restroom, the nurse with a pronounced accent, apparently African, yelled at me. As cited earlier in this book, I retorted, "Don't you yell at me like I'm a two-year-old." I made it back to the bed, where she angrily attended to me and left. Moments later, the supervisor passed by the room; I called him, but there was no response. I telephoned the nurse's station, but still there was no response. They totally ignored me!

I drifted off to sleep, which felt like a few minutes. Upon awakening, I called Lila on my cellphone. When she answered, my wife told me it was 5 a.m. and urgently wanted to know why I was calling. I told her about my experience and wanted out of this place. She calmed me and promised to arrange for my discharge.

The next night, a male nurse was assigned to care for me. To myself, I mused, "They sent the *goon squad* tonight and dared me to act out." Well, I was no fool. When I needed a Depend, an adult diaper, he came and gave me what I needed. He handled me somewhat roughly to let me know who was in charge. Oh, had this been B.C.—Before COVID—I believe that male nurse would have been surprised had he encountered a rather testosteronal 255-pound active preacher instead of a somewhat bedridden barely-able-to-walk-weakling patient, things would have been different. Thank God for grace and mercy.

Scant research about the Genesis Loch Raven Nursing Home, which changed to a rehabilitation facility in April 2020 and became open to receive COVID-19 patients, was revealing. FOX 45 WBFF on April 14, 2020, reported that three residents died at the facility. It was placed under quarantine. Baltimore County Councilman David Marks commented, "Simply put, Parkville has the worst outbreak in eastern Baltimore County," where the facility is located. The report disclosed that 27 residents and 17 employees tested positive for the virus. My roommate, Michael, died shortly after my admission to the facility.

The University of Maryland Charles Regional Medical Center had no other options for me because I was still testing positive for COVID-19, and the only facility with a vacancy that accepted COVID patients was the Genesis Loch Raven facility. Hence, I was transferred to the facility in Parkville, MD. My research revealed that there were mixed reviews about the rehabilitation place. Some comments were positive, while in contrast, some statements were made that paralleled my experience. Whatever the reasons are for the staff who performed their duties in the manner in which they did cannot be explained. Some were very caring and compassionate, and they brought with them moments of sunshine. Because of this, I am grateful to God.

Five years later, with keener insight, the traumatic experience in the rehabilitation facility seared into my memory as a violent storm at night. It is because of what happened there that I urge families and ministers to make regular visits to those who are in nursing homes and rehabilitation facilities, be very attentive, listen to the residents, and advocate on their behalf if necessary.

Hospitalizations have occurred for me since April 2020, lasting from a brief overnight stay to four days. My medical problems were related to cardiovascular and respiratory matters. Also, several in-and-out procedures were conducted at George Washington University Hospital, Washington, DC, and at The Johns Hopkins Hospital in Baltimore, Maryland. Through it all, I continue to thank God for healing mercies upon my body.

The death of Mother Margaret during our hospitalization for COVID-19 deepened the grief for my wife and me, especially since we had already lost our youngest son, Christopher, in May 2018. Both my wife and I speak about Mother and find ourselves speaking of her in the present; it is not uncommon for us to refer to her bedroom as "Mother's room." Our grief, in addition to that of other families experiencing the same, is not unlike many in the church where we attend and maintain my conference connection (with the United Methodist Church). To address the issue of grief, the Rev. Dr. Timothy West, senior pastor of Westphalia Christian Community Church, a United Methodist congregation, requested that I facilitate its *GriefShare* program. Since its inception at the church in the autumn of 2024, we have completed two cycles of thirteen sessions, with participants wanting additional sessions. To this end, we conducted an abbreviated summer session and are now entering our third full 13-week cycle for the fall of 2025.

Members of Westphalia Christian Community Church, affectionately known as *The W*, experienced the loss of loved ones due to the COVID-19 Global Pandemic, in addition to natural causes. Although it was five years later or less, on January 26, 2025, Dr. West delivered a much-needed message during a service of remembrance for the church and those who continued to mourn their loss. He compassionately spoke on "A Mighty Cloud of Witness" (Hebrews 12:1-2), especially to those who continued to have lingering issues of grief. At the conclusion of the pastor's message, Teresa B., a member of our *GriefShare* ministry, wearing her backpack, proceeded from the rear of the sanctuary, center aisle, to the altar. She pulled cardboard boxes from her backpack, symbolizing bricks with inscribed grief issues on the sides: anger, isolation, regrets, and one of the bricks sighted the unending sentiment, *if only* ..., and other grief issues, and placed them on the altar before the cross. The pastor invited members to come forth for prayer. It was an inspirational and powerful moment in which the church, and particularly members who were unable to mourn the loss of their loved ones publicly, came together as a community. Moreover, some grievers who were present had not been in worship for several years. With the help of the Holy Spirit, the brick-burdens were somewhat lightened as each griever continued to navigate their journey through grief.

I reflect on the experiences that occurred during the five-year period since I contracted the coronavirus and its traumatic impact on the lives of so many others. While negating being a predestinarian along with the associated theological constructs of the said perspective, I agree with the apostle Paul in his letter to the Roman Christians, "We know that all things work together for good for those who love God, who are called according to his purpose" (Romans 8:28). Indeed, some good did come out of our global COVID-19 pandemic experience. We were forced to acknowledge that the world does not operate in silos and that our lives are dependent upon one another. The limited availability of routine healthcare measures and the drastic shortages of toilet paper, disinfectants, and infant formulas worked to prove that.

And it became necessary for us to share with others the goodness of God in our lives. Again, I offer the testimony of Paul, "We do not want you to be unaware, brothers and sisters, of the affliction we experienced … for we were so utterly, unbearably crushed that we despaired of life itself … we felt that we had received the sentence of death, so that we would rely not on ourselves but on God who raises the dead. He who rescued us from so deadly a peril" (2 Corinthians 1: 8-10). I am thankful to God for God's indescribable gift of love expressed through grace and mercy.

CHAPTER 8

# A PRAXIS OF PRECAUTION

"A prudent person foresees danger and takes precautions"
(Proverbs 22:3 NLT)

The COVID-19 Global Pandemic occurred five years ago, leaving a traumatic impact upon the world. Our social order dramatically changed in every sphere of life. In the employment arena, workers in commercial, government, and some various industries were allowed to stay at home to perform their duties with the periodic requirement to report in person at the worksite. Social gatherings for entertainment narrowed their events to the virtual world.

Hospitals, the battlegrounds against COVID-19, instituted prevention measures to stop the spread of the deadly disease. A plethora of precautionary practices were implemented, such as restrictions on visitations. Craig J. Renner, director of Marketing and Communications and Director of Community Health, University of Maryland University System, informed that The University of Maryland Charles Regional Medical Center put into effect levels of visitation according to a system of color-coding: green, yellow, orange, and red, with green being the least and red being the most restricted. The system remained in force from March 2020 to September 2022. Anecdotally, even today, as a lingering precaution, it is not uncommon to see signage in conspicuous places in reference to the optional use of face masks.

In the world of academia, elementary, middle, and high schools opted to use virtual means for conducting classes. Colleges and universities followed in a similar manner with online classes. Further, commencement exercises were restricted to students graduating virtually. I recall a local high school in Charles County, MD, where a youth member of my church received his diploma in the school's parking lot. His parents sat in their car as their child went forth in his cap and gown with other students wearing face masks, receiving their diplomas. Such were the changes triggered by the Pandemic.

The issue of getting vaccinations and wearing face coverings is a no-brainer, in my opinion. My wife and I are vaccinated annually for coronavirus variants, flu, and pneumonia at local pharmacies, i.e., CVS or Giant, in addition to the Charles County, MD Health Department satellites, with the most recent vaccination taking place in September 2025. My wife and I wear NK-95 masks everywhere and take the prescribed/recommended preventative measures against airborne germs by hand washing thoroughly. We practice the said measures in view of our weakened immune systems and advanced age.

The church, as a composite observation, was no exception, as multiple changes and restrictions were enacted. Congregations with security protocols implemented and/or modified their standard operating procedures or toolkits. For example, greeters with face masks were equipped with digital thermometers to check the temperatures of people wanting to enter the church for worship services. Greeters were the first line of defense to prevent the further spread of the virus. If the temperatures of church members and visitors presented an acceptable range, they were permitted entrance. On the contrary, possibly infected persons were graciously denied entrance. In addition, congregants were required to register in advance via telephone call or online, days before attending scheduled worship services. Moreover, only a specific number of attendees with current vaccination cards were allowed into the church for worship.

Also, the worship ministry reflected change because of the pandemic. Choirs were reduced in number, with each choir member appropriately spaced as a precautionary measure against the potential spread of the coronavirus. Once a selection was finished, the choir members put their masks back on.

The worship team, consisting of a liturgist and preacher, wore masks and used their own microphones. The pulpit chairs, once positioned next to each other, were repositioned at opposite ends of the pulpit. When the liturgist finished speaking, he or she wiped the lectern and returned to their seat, still holding on to their microphone. The pastor/speaker also used their own microphone. This was the practice in certain churches during and immediately following the gradual lessening of COVID-19 restrictions.

Only a certain number of people were permitted during in-person worship services. Seating was spaced out in terms of leaving every other row of pews vacant. Certain colors of tape, red and green, were used to designate which row of seats was restricted or open. Red tape indicated the row was not to be used, while green indicated it was available for seating. Individuals were urged to sit six feet apart from one another unless they were family.

Worship materials, such as Bibles, hymnals, attendance cards for visitors, pens, pencils, and offering envelopes, were removed to prevent the spread of contamination. Worship through giving was another potential way to spread the deadly coronavirus; therefore, churches began to use online platforms, if not already in use, while still providing the opportunity for attendees to give their offerings in person. Ushers with face coverings in some faith communities continued to receive offerings by way of plates or baskets. Moreover, electronic giving was highly encouraged, as opposed to the use of physical gifts, though not discouraged. Pastor Kenneth Morrow Jones commented, "Church attendance was at a minimum due to quarantine restrictions ... However, somehow financial support started coming in."[1] Nevertheless, all was done to prevent the spread of the infectious and deadly coronavirus.

The time for the kerygma, the proclamation of the Lord, Jesus Christ as Savior, i.e., preaching, was the moment when the pastor/preacher removed his/her mask to proclaim the message of salvation through Jesus Christ. After the message, the invitation to Christian discipleship was offered. If there was a response to the invitation to join the church, the pastor, with a face covering re–adorned, came from the pulpit to floor level to receive the respondent. In other congregations, the respondent was directed to certain laypersons who met with them individually to provide the necessary information for joining the church.

Pertinent to sacred rituals, baptism, and holy communion, there were modifications. For baptisms, especially among United Methodists and, in particular, infant baptism, pastors were extra cautious. Not only were hands well sanitized, but face coverings were also mandated for the mutual protection of the child being baptized and their extended family members. Moreover, certain pastors only allowed the parents and the child to be brought forth for the sacred ceremony.

Holy Communion was another sacrament that required modification. Whereas in some churches, the altar was where the elements were openly positioned and made available for congregants to receive their communion. They could come right up and kneel at the altar rail. Communion stewards or altar guild members were present to handle the elements during the ritual; however, COVID-19 dictated that open elements could no longer be utilized. Rather, the single-unit cup with a small wafer sealed on top of a sealed cup containing the juice or wine would now be used. A number of senior members, including myself, at times struggled to open the small communion cup—thank God for my wife, who was much more nimble with her fingers and able to manipulate the sealings on the cup. The communion cups were distributed at the sanctuary's entrance by greeters and communion stewards before service. After communion service, the used cups were placed in disposable plastic bags held by ushers wearing sanitary gloves at the entrance of the sanctuary while congregants exited.

In decades gone by, many communion rituals actually featured a common loaf of bread and a cup of wine or juice, from which the entire congregation partook. From my observation, communion by intinction is not practiced as it used to be in some worship settings. This is not to suggest that I prefer it the old way, because changes to the original practices have proven more beneficial and protective for the masses in this context of time.

Another precautionary change in the order of worship was the foregoing of the traditional recessional of the choir, the pastor, and the pulpit staff. Pre-COVID-19, many would expect to meet and greet the pastor after the service heartily.

During the emergence of the coronavirus, to battle the onset of new cases, at the close of the service, featuring the benediction or a sending-forth prayer, the choir remained in place, the liturgist exited by the side aisle, and the pastor often left by way of the center aisle. In some congregations, the benediction was spoken from the pulpit, after which the pastor exited to the pulpit's adjoining room. Meanwhile, worshipers were dismissed by aisle and directed to leave the church immediately. There was no gathering in the outside hall or narthex areas, where worshipers fellowshipped with handshaking and hugs. The pastor or minister did not interact with the parishioners after the service. Again, it was a practice of precaution to avoid the spread of COVID-19.

Today, five years and counting, the traditions of how congregants leave a church service have returned to a semblance of pre-COVID-19 norms.

Essentially, in my observation, the limitations put on the number of people allowed to attend worship services in person unintentionally engendered a sterility of fellowship, as many chose to view the services virtually. Furthermore, I contend that behavior has evolved to the point where people prefer to engage in virtual worship. I believe that a study is needed that pertains to the dramatic impact of COVID-19, which has changed the behavior of many worshipers who now opt to view church services virtually rather than reengaging in person.

The relaxation of COVID-19 restrictions enabled churches to gradually reopen their doors for in-person worship. From my observations, while some parishioners slowly returned to the sanctuary, a certain population of church members still prefers virtual worship services. The question is why? And I do not believe that the answer is simply a matter of convenience. The point is that for many, there may be unaddressed levels of trauma and grief affecting their choices. In fact, an editorial opinion cited according to a news release from the National

Alliance on Mental Health Issues (NAMI) pointed to the effects of the COVID-19 Global Pandemic on so many people. The mental health condition during the first year of the Pandemic rose from an annual rate of 1 in 5 Americans to 2 in 5 or higher, according to NAMI.[2]

That said, during a virtual Bible study with a colleague, one of the participants offered, "I can go to morning service while in my pajamas in my den and have my coffee, too!" That comment of the participant was reflective of the sentiments of many and indicative of a paradigm shift in the way *we do church*. Moreover, while a wider audience of viewers can be reached, a greater degree of sterility of fellowship is in the making. An electronic band or wave is keeping us connected. But is iso lationism becoming part of the church's experience over and against ecclesial? Most mental health professionals consider isolationism a mental health issue within various segments of the population.

The impact of the COVID-19 Global Pandemic continues as an echo from a dark storm that caused certain practices to become our new norms. It is not uncommon to see persons in worship with face coverings. Bibles and hymnals are often no longer in pew racks, in addition to paper bulletins distributed by ushers. Now, big screens convey announcements, scriptures, and song lyrics. Often, bulletins are sent ahead of time to church members online. There is a conspicuous display of hand sanitizers throughout the church, along with signage encouraging the washing of hands. While the church continues a praxis of precaution, thanks be to God, it also continues in its praxis of delivering the redemptive message of salvation through Jesus Christ, our Lord and Savior, who will return —i.e., the kerygma.

The praxis of precaution is strongly emphasized in the Old Testament's Levitical legislation of the Bible, such as in Leviticus 21:1-4 and Numbers 19:11-13, 16. The legislation provided procedures for the priests and the people on how to handle themselves and the deceased.

The New Testament's John 11 offers us a profound insight into grief and mourning amongst a first-century family—the death of Lazarus.

The devastating impact of the COVID-19 Global Pandemic was profoundly demonstrated in the funeral industry. Funeral establishments complied with local, state, and federal laws and guidelines promulgated by the Center for Disease Control pertinent to family viewings and funeral services. In addition, individual funeral companies, while supporting the needs of bereaved families, encouraged those who desired to support the families to practice social distancing based upon public health directives. The companies were emphatic about wearing face masks and recommended best practices to prevent the spread of the deadly Coronavirus. The funeral companies, in view of the Pandemic, continued to plan traditional services as much as possible.

The Africanism of community celebration of life for a deceased member influences the traditional African American religious funeral practices. The said tradition is expressed through open joyous celebrations during funeral services, i.e., Celebration of Life or Homegoing Services. Regardless of whether there was a wake (viewing) or main service, the celebrative event, while in the midst of grief, was conducted with the gathered community. However, the COVID-19 Global Pandemic interrupted the way friends and neighbors came together to celebrate and honor the life of a decedent.

Mrs. Tanja Carter, executive assistant and niece of the late Leon Thornton, owner of the Thornton Funeral Home, PA, Indian Head, Maryland, commented on the effects of the COVID-19 Global Pandemic upon their company. Their company assiduously complied with the standards of the Occupational Safety and Health Administration

(OSHA) to ensure that a safe working environment was maintained for their employees as they cared for the deceased, time of removal, funeral service (if requested, because some families opted to only have graveside services), to cremation or interment.

Mrs. Carter detailed further effects of COVID-19 on their funeral service. She said:

"Fewer to no families wanted limousine service, nor did funeral homes want to provide the service. A group of nine contained in a small space sharing the same oxygen possibly spreading the virus was enough of a deterrent to stop the use. Families riding in limousines together to arrive at the church or funeral home was part of the tradition. This sense of community was taken away during COVID-19."

Mrs. Carter opined that by not using limousine service, certain emotional and social customs were negated on the day of the funeral service that:

- Provided a sense of unity and togetherness during a difficult time.
- Offered a private space for family members to share memories and emotions.
- Symbolized respect and dignity for the deceased.
- Ensured everyone arrives at the service together, avoiding delays.
- Reduced the stress of navigating transportation logistics on a sad day.
- Allowed for a more comfortable and supportive environment for grieving.

Another aspect that the executive assistant addressed was the community support for the family. She continued to mention about the diminished support from friends and neighbors for the bereaved family.

COVID-19 significantly hindered the public with the opportunity to show the worth of the deceased. For a period, families were limited to having a service (if one was provided) of no more than ten, twenty-five, or fifty people. This was disruptive and disturbing, especially when the immediate family had more than ten people in it. The late Mr. Thornton's niece contended:

- Provided an opportunity for family and friends to say their final goodbyes.
- Allowed attendees to pay their respects and offer condolences to the grieving family.
- Created a space for shared memories and stories about the deceased.
- Helped individuals process their grief in a supportive environment.
- Offered a chance to celebrate the life and legacy of the person who has passed.
- Served as a cultural or religious tradition that held significance for the family.

Mrs. Carter discussed the matter of the repast that followed funeral services. She said, "COVID eliminated the repast," and offered the following justifications for the value of the after-funeral meal:

- A Place for Comfort: The repast gives people a chance to comfort one another and feel supported.
- Remembering Together: Sharing stories and memories of the person who has passed helps keep their legacy alive.
- Symbol of Togetherness: Eating together reminds everyone that life goes on and that they are not alone in their grief.

An issue of significance was the high incidence of deaths during the COVID-19 Global Pandemic, which caused a delay in burying the deceased. There was not enough space to shelter the decedents in the mortuary because of the backup at the local cemeteries, especially the local Maryland Veterans Cemetery, Cheltenham, Maryland. (In the funeral industry, the word *sheltering* means storage of deceased remains, particularly refrigeration storage.)

Finally, it was Mrs. Tanja Carter's opinion that families did not get community support during the COVID-19 Global Pandemic, thereby isolating them from being able to adequately share their grief.

Now, five years-plus removed from the occurrence of the COVID-19 Global Pandemic, there have been some important changes in the funeral industry. Nationwide, during the period 2021-2022, restrictions were lifted while still maintaining precautionary measures because of variants of the virus. The Thornton Funeral Home, PA, while not jeopardizing their compliance with OSHA, relaxed some of its restrictions to pre-pandemic levels. However, upon entrance to the funeral home, a conspicuous sign indicates the highly recommended use of face masks while simultaneously stating that it is optional. Mrs. Carter offered that when families of recently deceased people meet for service arrangements, the conference room is sanitized once the meeting is over as a precaution. Further, signage throughout their facility strongly stressed the wearing of face coverings or masks. It is not uncommon to see members of the community and/or family with face masks. Staff members also wear face masks and have hand sanitizers during gatherings for the convenience of attendees.

The guest book in the lobby of the funeral home has receptacles for new and used writing instruments, along with hand sanitizers, all for the purpose of preventing the spread of germs. Service programs are distributed by greeters or staff members of the funeral home, again to reduce the spread of germs.

There is now an increase in the use of technology in the funeral industry. The Pandemic necessitated the use of online meetings, live-streaming, and obituaries on websites, to mention a few. Anecdotally, Jock Schofield, our nephew, who is very savvy with electronic gadgetry, was permitted to live-stream the funeral service at the Howell Funeral Home, Baltimore, Maryland, for our beloved Mother Margret in April 2020, while I was in rehab for my recovery from COVID-19. I saw the recorded service when I returned home during the latter part of May 2020. The funeral director was very impressed with what our nephew produced; as a result, he was contracted to live-stream for the company at all its locations. That was five years ago as of this writing.

We are five years past the horrendous COVID-19 Global Pandemic, although many of us continue to suffer from traumatic emotional, mental, and physical wounds. Our societal institutions endeavored to promulgate policies, procedures, and protocols as proactive measures to prevent the further spread of the coronavirus and its variants. To this end, precautionary measures such as sanitizing our spaces and ourselves are highly encouraged. The wearing of face coverings, safe distancing, and social intercourse such as handshaking, hugging, and indiscriminate kissing are not as spontaneous as it was in pre-pandemic times. Although there is an unhurried return to pre-pandemic social norms, the praxis of precaution remains very prevalent.

## CHAPTER 9

# COLLATERAL BLESSINGS, FIVE YEARS LATER

"We know that all things work together for good for those
who love God, who are called according to his purpose"
(Romans 8:28)

Many years ago, I preached, "Good Comes Out of Bad Situations,"
which addressed the rise of drug infestation in a Laurel, MD
community where my local church, St. Mark's United Methodist
Church, was situated. From the sermon, we organized *Orange Hat Patrols*, derisively called *Pumpkin Heads*, and began unannounced patrols
in the immediate community. The church members, mainly the men
of the church, along with a few women, took shifts throughout the
night. We were equipped with donated walkie-talkies and orange hats.

Any possible drug activity was reported, and the local police came
swiftly. On one such occasion, I chased a certain low-level drug dealer
who escaped me by running through a nearby wooded area. I had
formerly served in law enforcement, so the old adrenaline kicked in,

causing me to give an initial chase, minus my more youthful stride of the old days. Stopping short of that wooded area, my common sense also kicked in. While I did not catch that low-level drug dealer, he was eventually arrested, convicted, and served a term of imprisonment. But the story did not end there.

Years later, that same low-level drug dealer accepted Jesus Christ as his Savior. He was authentically transformed by the saving grace of God while in prison. Not long after, he sensed a call to Christian ministry, was ordained in the Baptist church, and now serves as pastor of a local church in the community where he once sold drugs! Throughout the years, we kept in touch; I continued to mentor him, and as pastor, I invited him to preach for me while I served Metropolitan United Methodist Church in Indian Head, MD.

Rev. Devan Hebron, pastor of the New Life Church of Christ in Laurel, MD, shared with the members of Metropolitan his account of my chasing him and escaping me, only to be caught by Jesus Christ. The once local drug pusher had his Damascus Road experience while incarcerated, which authentically changed him to become a servant of God. Today, he is a friend and colleague who serves a vital congregation in the Laurel community where our paths initially crossed. The foregoing account is a testimony to the transformative power of God's grace and mercy, serving as agency for causing collateral blessings.

The founder and pastor of Refreshing Life Christian Center in Chicago, Illinois, Pastor Kenneth Murrow Jones, also defines collateral blessings. He says, "[the] term ... suggests positive outcomes or benefits that arise indirectly or unexpectedly from a particular situation and or action. It implies that while the primary focus may be on one aspect, some additional advantages and consequences accompany it."[1] He continued, "It emphasizes the idea that even in difficult times, or in the face of a tragic loss, there can be gains ... blessings waiting to be discovered."[2]

It is now five years since the death of my mother-in-law, who succumbed to COVID-19 while we were in the same quarantine area of the ICU in the University of Maryland Charles Regional Medical Center, and where I miraculously recovered. I do not question God, but I thank God daily for His grace and mercy, allowing me to live while so many others died. I experienced the grace and healing mercy as did King Hezekiah (2 Kings 20:1-11; 2 Chronicles 32:24-26; Isaiah 38). I take each day as a blessing from God and a day of thanksgiving. I am not silent about God sparing my life.

The collateral blessings manifested in many unexpected ways. My resignation from Smith Chapel United Methodist Church caused a lot of grief in my spirit. While I wanted to hold on to the pastoral leadership of the congregation, I knew it was time for me to leave as pastor due to my incapacity because of COVID-19. It was painful, but I recalled from the Holy Scriptures that there is a season and a time for everything under the heaven (Ecclesiastes 3:1).

My successor was a young, anointed servant of God, Keith White, and he possessed the energy needed for the ministry of the church. In fact, our son and daughter-in-love, who regularly came to worship service once a month after my leaving the pastorate at Smith Chapel United Methodist Church, became full members! From being obliged to support their elderly parents in ministry to becoming faithful members of Christ Jesus' church while using their gifts and graces to the glory of God was a blessing. Anecdotally, our son gave the morning prayer during the Mother's Day Service at Smith Chapel UMC ... What a collateral blessing!

I reflect upon the many saints of God who prayed for my recovery, due to the mortality rate during the early months of COVID-19 not being favorable (understatement). As an African American male, then 77 years old with a compromised immune system, related to my military service many years ago, the probability of my survival was doubtful. A social worker in the hospital labelled me a miracle because 80 percent of those who entered the ICU did not survive, hence, *Miraculous.*

Countless numbers of times over the years, I had preached of God, who was able to do the impossible, and that God heard the prayers of the saints. Lila, my wife, received many calls from people who encouraged her by letting her know that they were praying for me. As mentioned earlier, Mrs. Gwendolyn B. Kent, widow of my colleague, the late Rev. Dr. Otto Kent, and Mrs. Stephanie West, the wife of Rev. Dr. Timothy West, pastor of Westphalia Christian Community Church, Upper Marlboro, MD, called and covenanted to fast and pray with Lila for my recovery. Because of their faithfulness in fasting and praying with Mrs. DeFord, when I was fully recovered, we became a part of Westphalia. (Retired United Methodist pastors in full membership do not join local churches because we are members of the Annual Conference; we maintain our connections with local churches, which is referred to as our "Charge Conference.")

Because of the fasting and prayers of Mrs. Gwendolyn B. Kent and Mrs. Stephanie West, along with my wife, the ladies organized a daily prayer team known as the *Prayer and Praise Warriors* (PPW). Mrs. Johanna Coleman also joined with the ladies in their prayer ministry. Prayer intercessions, petitions, and supplications are daily uttered on behalf of the church, affectionately nicknamed by its members, *The W*. The PPW enhances those efforts, which cover the church's ministries, the community, and all identified concerns. The ladies of PPW, who also pray for one another, could be considered as an adjunct to the Pastor's weekly prayer service. The foregoing is another example of God's provision of collateral blessings.

Other new ministry opportunities have opened to me in the five years since my bout with COVID-19. The Reverend Eugene Matthews, former district superintendent, a retired member who served several churches, checked on me regularly before my intubation in ICU. Rev. Matthews invited me to preach a few times between 2021 and early 2024. Moreover, the Rev. Dr. Johnsie Cogman, District Superintendent of the Southern Region, called upon me to fill in at a few churches in addition to Metropolitan United Methodist Church, one of my former appointments. Additionally, Rev. Dr. Timothy West periodically called upon me to preach in his absence, with the most recent preaching event during the Ash Wednesday Service of 2025.

Most significantly, however, upon the recommendation of Dr. Timothy West, I facilitated the church's *GriefShare* Ministry, while also serving as a teacher for the Senior Adult Bible Study. This Grief Ministry, held via Zoom, attracted participants from as far away as Tampa, Florida, to Northern Maryland. Some members who stayed away from the church because of their grief issues returned because of learning ways to navigate through their grief. When placing their experiences in perspective, it was God's transforming of difficult and overwhelming situations to God's glory. I am reminded of Marvin Williams' words, "When adversity comes, let's trust God's perspective and believe that—even from what's difficult—He can bring something good."[3] Collateral blessings are evident.

The occasion of my discharge from the University of Maryland Charles Regional Medical Center on May 8, 2020, had media coverage, along with a far-reaching impact not only on my immediate family, friends, acquaintances, and local community, but also on those who were key to my recovery. Admittedly, and in retrospect, I thought that the celebratory discharge was part of the hospital protocol for a job well done by the staff. However, it was not until Lila and I met two of the medical staff, Mary Hannah, VP Population Health and Case Management, and Teri White, Transitional Nurse and Navigator, who were participating in a writers' workshop held at the medical center, facilitated by the Life Journeys Writers Guild, on June 18, 2025. Both nurses remembered us and the time of my discharge. We all embraced one another and eventually took photographs in the very same hallway of the hospital where many medical team members had lined up on both sides five years earlier, as I was discharged from the hospital. Ms. White gave me her contact information.

I took the opportunity on July 29, 2025, during a phone conversation to get information for inclusion in the extended edition of our book. Ms. Teri White shared with me the emotional "traumatic time" that overwhelmed the medical team. "People were just dropping … in nursing homes … we never had seen anything like this before … everyone was so sick, and we locked down," said Nurse White. According to Teri, families could not be with their loved ones. "Everyone had on their moon suits; you could not see their faces, but you could see their eyes …," said the nurse. She continued, "It was a solemn mood."

Nurse White went on to explain that due to the gravity of the growing number of COVID-19 patients and the strain on the staff, she left the educational area of nursing to volunteer to assist with serving online with overworked nurses. "It was overwhelmingly exhausting" and emotionally draining for the medical teams.

Teri White mentioned the ripple effect on the families of the medical team members. After returning home from their shifts, they had to completely change their clothing to prevent carrying any contaminants from the coronavirus. Family members were concerned about being infected. And the cycle repeated, going to the hospital, another long shift in moon suits, treating patients, losing the battle with the deadly virus, and another death. It was demoralizing. It was painful. It seemed hopeless.

The reality of those moon suits that the staff had to adorn meant that it was the last thing a dying patient saw, instead of being surrounded by the presence of loved ones.

Nurse White said to me, "I remember the day you left. We saw you. It was so emotional to see you leave and your wife kiss [you] and not want to let you go. That day, you gave us hope because we did not know much about this virus." Moreover, she expressed that it was good to see and hear the patient's view.

The miraculous blessing was my physical recovery during the early phase of the COVID-19 Global Pandemic, in addition to the collateral blessings of the medical staff members, who, through their traumatically emotional and exhausting experiences, were able to witness the recovery of a patient with an apparent doubtful prognosis. It was a cathartic moment for them.

The COVID-19 Global Pandemic continues to echo like a dark storm with its aftermath of trauma upon the world. Yet, hope remains. Recalling my ministry during the early 1980s at St. Mark's United Methodist Church, I preached the sermon, titled *Good Out of a Bad Situation*, based upon the apostle's letter to the Roman Christian, "We know all things work together for good for those who love God, who are called according to his purpose" (Romans 8:28). Many of the old saints of that era have gone on to be with God, but the word of God continues to stand forever. I continue to be optimistic, even in the current political storm in our country. I wholeheartedly agree with the prayer: "Heavenly Father, please use my challenging moments to bring out Your will in my life."[4] I look for more collateral blessings despite the challenging vicissitudes of life.

## CHAPTER 10

# CLOSING THOUGHTS

"Finally, brothers and sisters, farewell. Put things in order,
listen to my appeal, agree with one another, live in peace;
and the God of love and peace will be with you"
(2 Corinthians 13:11)

The apostle Paul, in his final correspondence to the Corinthian
church, which had become distrustful of him and his ministry,
concludes his message of love and admonition. He urges them to
eliminate the disorder that occurred and pay attention to his advice,
rather than being so spiritually opinionated. With a flavoring of Psalm
133, he desires that the congregation should live in peace and harmony
with one another, guaranteeing a sense of community shalom.

Our hope is that this memoir will be of help to you and your loved
ones. We were candid and gave a glimpse into the traumatic impact
upon our lives as a pastoral family during the sickening effects of the
deadly virus. Because, as servants of the Lord Jesus Christ, we, just like
other non-immunized individuals, were as vulnerable to the COVID-19
consequences as anyone else who had not yet been immunized. The

saints of old told us that just because you accepted Christ as your Lord and Savior, such did not mean you would never have rough roads to traverse in your lives. Thus, we took an hourglass look-see at our life-changing journey both in real time and five years later.

Our hope was and continues to be that the coronavirus will be treated not as a hoax perpetrated by any political party, but as a very deadly disease that could rear its ugly head, uncontrollable, at any given time. The virus is no respecter of age, ethnicity, political affiliation, economic or social status. It has an open season on humanity. Yet, we hope that with the utilization of proven medical methodologies and protocols, Americans will continue to survive this Goliathan specter, so that we can share the sentiments of the psalmist, "I shall not die, but shall live and recount the deeds of the Lord" (Psalm 118:17).

God continues to be a miracle-working God. The Lord is a healer (Jehovah Rapha) and the Lord is merciful (Jehovah Rahum). The hymnologist put it, "I will trust in the Lord, I will trust in the Lord 'til I die."[1]

It is our steadfast hope that this memoir provides probative value to the reader, serving as a source of encouragement and affirmation that God is with us in both our best moments and as we navigate through our darkest valleys. It is this affirmation that shapes our character and solidifies our faith in Jesus Christ. God miraculously heals by God's own intervention and/or through the wisdom given to medical professionals and scientists to apply to the myriads of patients for their healing and recovery. And lest we never forget how the positive attitudes of patients, along with the fasting and praying of their supporters, activate the healing balm needed for their miraculous recoveries.

Beloved, hold on to God's unchanging hand. God is a miracle-working God.

*"A miracle is God doing what only God can do."*[2]

# REFERENCES

Chapter 1

1, 2, 3, and 4 David J. Sencer, CDC Museum: In Association with Smithsonian Institution,

5, and 6 Nature.com, April 15, 2020.

7.  Reuben P. Job, Norman Shawchuck, *A Guide to Prayer for Ministers and Other Servants,* In-text citation, *From Something Beautiful for God by Malcom Muggeridge,* The Upper Room Books, Nashville, Tennessee, 1993, p. 370.

Chapter 2

1.  Herbert Lockyer, *All the Miracles of the Bible,* Zondervan Books, Zondervan Publishing House, Grand Rapids, Michigan, 1961, p. 15.

2.  Ibid., p. 13.

3.  *The New Interpreter's Dictionary of the Bible, Me-R Volume 4,* Abingdon Press, Nashville, 2009, p. 100.

4.  Ibid., p. 104.

5.  *The New Interpreter's Bible: A Commentary in Twelve Volumes, Volume VIII, New Testament Articles: Matthew, Mark,* Abingdon Press, Nashville, 1995, p. 248.

6. Edwards, Brian H. *"Best Inspirational Quotes on Miracles,"* graceousquotes.com.

7. *The Book of Discipline of The United Methodist Church, 2016,* The United Methodist Publishing House, Nashville, Tenn., p. 270.

8. Shane Claiborne, Jonathan Wilson-Hartgrove, Enuma Okoro, *Common Prayer A Liturgy For Ordinary Radicals,* Zondervan, Grand Rapids, Michigan, 2010, p. 411.

9. Philip Yancey, *Prayer: Does it Make Any Difference?* Zondervan, Grand Rapids, Michigan, 2006, p.163.

10. Herbert Lockyear, *All the Prayers of the Bible,* Zondervan, Grand Rapids, Michigan, 1959.

11. Elmer L. Towns, *Fasting for Spiritual Break Through: A Guide to Nine Biblical Fasts,* Regal Books from Gospel Light, Ventura California, 1996, p. 23.

12. Ibid, pp. 23-24.

13. *The New Interpreter's Dictionary of the Bible D-H Volume 2,* Abingdon Press, Nashville, 2007, p.755.

Chapter 4

1. Norman Cousins, *Anatomy of An Illness: As Perceived by the Patient,* W.W. Norton & Company, New York, 1979, p.151.

Chapter 6

1. Norman Cousins, *Anatomy of An Illness: As Perceived by the Patient,* W.W. Norton & Company, New York, 1979, p. 13.

2. Ibid, p. 49.

3. *The Upper Room January—February 2021,* Bezalie Bautista Ue-Kung, "Hope in Suffering," The Upper Room, Nashville, TN, p.25.

4. Ibid., p. 25.

Chapter 7

1. Carla A. Grosch Miller, *Trauma and Pastoral Care: A Ministry Handbook,* Canterbury Press, London ECIY OTG, UK, 2021, pp. 3-4.

Chapter 8

1. Kenneth Morrow Jones, *Collateral Blessings: A Journey to Recovery, Hope, and Inspiration During Difficult Times,* Flaming Sword Productions, Middletown, DE, 27 April 2025, p. 37.
2. National Alliance on Mental Health Issues (NAMI).

Chapter 9

1. Kenneth Morrow Jones, *Collateral Blessings: A Journey to Recovery, Hope, and Inspiration During Difficult Times,* Flaming Sword Productions, Middletown, DE, 27 April 2025, p. 13.
2. Ibid., p. 13.
3. Marvin Williams, *"God's Perspective,"* Our Daily Bread, Sunday, *May 3, 2025.*
4. Ibid.

Chapter 10

1. United Methodist Hymnal, *"I Will Trust in the Lord,"* The United Methodist Publishing House, Nashville, Tennessee, 1989, p. 464.
2. Dunn, Ronald, *"Best Inspirational Quotes,"* graceousquotes.com

# BIBLIOGRAPHY

*Claiborne, Shane, Jonathan Wilson-Wilson, Enuma Okoro. *Common Prayer A Liturgy for Ordinary Radicals*. Grand Rapids, Michigan, Zondervan, 2010.

*Cousins, Norman. *Anatomy of An Illness: As Perceived by the Patient*. New York, W. W. Norton & Company, 1979.

*Dunn, Ronald. *Best Inspirational Quotes*, graceousquotes.com.

*Edwards, Brian H. *Best Inspirational Quotes on Miracles*, graceousquotes.com.

*Job, Reuben P., and Norman Shawchuck. *A Guide to Prayer for Ministers and Other Servants*, in text citation, *From Something Beautiful for God* by Malcolm Muggeridge, Nashville, Tennessee, The Upper Room Books, 1993.

*Jones, Kenneth Morrow, *Collateral Blessings: A Journey to Recovery, Hope, and Inspiration During Difficult Times*, Flaming Sword Productions, Middletown, DE, 27 April 2025.

*Keck, Leander E. Convener and Senior New Testament Editor. *The Interpreter's Bible: A Commentary in Twelve Volumes, Volume VIII, New Testament Articles: Matthew, Mark*, Nashville, Abingdon Press, 1995.

*Lockyer, Herbert. *All the Prayers of the Bible*, Zondervan Books, Zondervan Publishing House, Grand Rapids, Michigan, 1959. *All the Miracles of the Bible*, Zondervan Books, Zondervan Publishing House, Grand Rapids, Michigan, 1961.

* *The Book of Discipline of The United Methodist Church, 2016*, Nashville, Tennessee, The United Methodist Publishing House, 2016.

*Sakenfeld, Katharine Doob, General Editor. *The New Interpreter's Dictionary of the Bible D—H, Volume 2*, Nashville, Abingdon Press, 2007. *The New Interpreter's Dictionary of the Bible, Me—R, Volume 4*, Nashville, Nashville, Abingdon Press, 2009.

*Towns, Elmer L. *Fasting for Spiritual Break Through: A Guide to Nine Biblical Fasts*, Ventura, California, Regal Books from Gospel Light, 1996.

* *The United Methodist Hymnal, I Will Trust in the Lord*, Nashville, Tennessee, The United Methodist Publishing House, 1989.

*Uc-Kung, Bezalie Bautista. *Hope in Suffering, The Upper Room, January-February 2021*, Nashville, Tennessee, The Upper Room.

# ABOUT THE AUTHORS

Rev. Dr. George and Mrs. Lila DeFord, whom he affectionately calls "his girlfriend and wife who is one and the same," make their home in Pomfret, Maryland. Together they have three adult sons, of whom the youngest son, deceased in May 2018, and two grandsons.

Rev. DeFord is a graduate of Morgan State, Coppin State, and Howard Universities. Mrs. DeFord graduated from the University of Maryland College Park and matriculated at Bowie State University for graduate studies.

After forty-three years of ordained ministry in the Baltimore-Washington Conference, The United Methodist Church, Rev. DeFord resigned from Smith Chapel UMC, LaPlata, MD, due to hospitalization and rehabilitation from COVID-19 infection.

**Other Books by Reverend Dr. George F. DeFord**

*Oh, My Child, My Child: The Dilemma of Clergy Confronting Personal Grief* (G. Franklin DeFord Publishing)

*Celebrating Life within the African-American Tradition* (Anointed Press Publishers)

*Experiences in Serving African American Churches in Context: Urban Suburban Rural* (Xulon Press)